NANCY AKHAVAN

Literacy Walks

A Collaborative Process to Transform Teaching and Learning Across the School Year

SCHOLASTIC

For Cinnamon Schuefele, principal,
and all learning facilitators at
Washington Elementary School in Lindsay
Unified School District in California.
I have learned so much from all of you.
Thank you for walking with me, making me
a better coach, and modeling for me exactly
how to be passionate about teaching.

Acquisitions editor: Lois Bridges
Editorial director: Sarah Longhi
Development editor: Raymond Coutu
Senior editor: Shelley Griffin
Production editor: Danny Miller
Designer: Maria Lilja

Photos ©: Cover: SolStock/Getty Images; back cover: Sayeh Akhavan; 7: wavebreakmedia/Shutterstock; 29: DGLimages/Shutterstock; 32: PATCHARIN SIMALHEK/Shutterstock; 37: AYA images/Shutterstock; 40: NDAB Creativity/Shutterstock; 63: Atstock Productions/Shutterstock. Icons by The Noun Project. All other photos courtesy of the author.

"Please Listen" from *Loving Each Other* by Leo Buscaglia. Copyright © 1984 by Leo Buscaglia. Used by permission of Slack Incorporated, Thorofare, NJ. All rights reserved.

ISBN 978-1-338-77019-3

Contents

PART I: BEFORE THE WALK
Seeing Schools as Communities of Practice

PART II: DURING THE WALK
Learning from Literacy Walks

PART III: AFTER THE WALK
Coaching to Improve Teacher and Student Learning

Acknowledgments

This book came about because of the many teachers and leaders who have a vision of learning together while walking classrooms. But that vision is only part of the process. Without the team at Scholastic, this book could not have become a reality. I would like to thank Michael Haggen for seeing the potential for the book. I would like to thank Ray Coutu and Sarah Longhi for launching me into writing it, and the rest of the editorial and design team for making the book beautiful: Shelley Griffin, Danny Miller, and Maria Lilja. I am most grateful to Ray who created the online look-for forms, which are integral to the book, and spent hours and hours aligning all the parts. Last but certainly not least, thank you to Lois Bridges who was an irreplaceable brainstorming partner. You all have lifted me up. Thank you so much. I am humbled.

Introduction

The power to solve problems of practice is within ourselves.

We can make change by learning together through short visits to one another's classrooms, where we observe what students are doing in response to instruction. And we can do that in any subject area, but my world revolves around literacy, and this book focuses specifically on observing literacy learning. Literacy walks are about learning in order to improve teaching and especially to improve students' learning. A literacy walk is a classroom visit that provides administrators and teachers an opportunity to reflect on what and how students are learning, how they engage with the content, and how they interact with the teacher and peers.

When I became a teacher, keeping my classroom door shut and not allowing anyone to watch me was the way things were done. Teaching was not transparent. I would have flat-out died if a group of teachers and a leader had walked into my room and stayed to talk with students about what they were doing. Surely, I knew I needed help. I was a new teacher, after all. But the unstated teaching code kept me quiet: Don't admit you need help! I did not want my vulnerability to show.

But I now know that having clarity in your teaching makes it much more likely your students will learn, which is one of the best reasons to conduct literacy walks. Walks help us to see our teaching clearly. Our colleagues observe us and collect notes to help us see our practice more clearly, and to understand what works best for our students' growth. When I was a new teacher, I know I would have benefited from the insights of my colleagues. This can happen during a literacy walk.

Literacy walks help us understand how we teach and what characteristics of our teaching lead to students' literacy achievement (Kelcey & Carlisle, 2013). We can teach to our heart's content, but if students aren't learning, then we are not truly teaching. The information we gather during a literacy walk helps us to clarify our teaching to meet our students' needs. Literacy walks also help us understand other aspects of instruction, such as:

- access to literacy materials and how those materials help students learn.
- quality of classroom climates.
- equitable access to instruction.
- types of texts available to students for literacy learning.

I have seen the power of teachers and administrators working together to understand how a lesson leads to student learning, and what the students know and can do because of either that lesson or previous lessons. Teaching at its core is a learning process; it's getting curious about *problems* and framing teaching as *problem-solving*. I invite you to dive into this book with colleagues, or even on your own. When you follow the steps I lay out in these pages, literacy walks are efficacious; you will be empowered to take ownership of your own professional learning and you can pave the way for changes in your classroom that would not have been possible without learning in partnership with your colleagues.

PART I
BEFORE THE WALK

Seeing Schools as Communities of Practice

CHAPTER 1

Literacy Walks
The Power of Collaboration

"I am excited when I see literacy walks on the school calendar. I enjoy working with my colleagues to improve how we are teaching so our students can learn more."

— JOSÉ, SECOND-GRADE TEACHER

Many (many) years ago, in my ninth year of teaching, I was part of a team that went on 10- to 15-minute visits to one another's classrooms to learn how well we were implementing small-group reading and how well students were responding to it. I remember the day my colleagues came to my room to observe me teach. I felt a mix of excitement and dread. I didn't want to look like I didn't know what I was doing, but I was also eager to find out what my colleagues noticed. Of course, I was just learning how to teach small-group reading, so there was really no way that I was not going to make a mistake. I had my turn to observe my colleagues, too. I watched how one of them, Julie, laid out small whiteboards for students to write a sentence. She swept her index finger across the board to show the students the direction to write. In the afternoon my team members and I gathered to discuss what we saw and learned. I learned that my practices were similar to Julie's, but she encouraged students in a way I didn't. I began to weave in more supportive gestures, such as that directional sweep I'd observed, in my own small-group work and noticed my students responding to my directions in a more focused way. It was life-changing because I realized that, together, by looking at and discussing our practices, we were becoming better teachers.

When we learn with colleagues about the art of our teaching, we take down, figuratively, our classroom walls. It gives us the power to lead our own learning, and to use data we collect to make decisions about our next steps. When we lead our own learning, we focus more closely on how we are teaching, and we are empowered to guide ourselves.

What a Literacy Walk Is

In a literacy walk, we visit one another's classrooms, taking clear and accurate notes about what teachers are doing and how students are working. Before a walk, team members set up a schedule to visit classrooms, and establish a focus for what they are going to notice and note. After the walk, they gather to debrief their notes, thoughts, and ideas.

Literacy walks provide opportunities for teachers, instructional coaches, and administrators to work together to support the growth of individual teachers, grade-level teachers, and the whole faculty (Moss & Borrkhart, 2015; Taylor & Chanter, 2019). They also provide opportunities for teachers and administrators to gain insight into effective literacy practices and for teams to decide for themselves what they need next in professional development (Kelcey & Carlisle, 2013; Kosanovich, Smith, Hensley, Osborne-Lampking, & Foorman, 2015). I've found that lasting, ground-up change is most likely when team members are open to investigating their practices and trying new solutions.

We can foster a growth mindset as we learn together about our students and ourselves. We can choose to stretch ourselves and "unfix" any static mindsets. Dweck (2007) says that stretching ourselves to learn something new is to develop ourselves. We must analyze situations with a growth mindset. According to Brooks and Goldstein (2008), our mindset directly relates to the effectiveness of our teaching strategies and the extent to which they impact student achievement. A growth mindset enables us to take on new processes and initiatives more positively (Goree & Akhavan, in press). Remember, *the power to solve our problems in the classroom is within ourselves.* As I describe literacy walks, I propose ways you can continue to grow in your teaching and ensure that your students are learning. This might be a small change, such as using more physical cues in instruction, or a big change, such as overhauling the way you structure conferences during independent reading.

I believe in literacy walks because they are a collegial, developmental, school-based approach to improving teaching and learning. They can help us recommend instruction that will improve student learning. As we discover ways to tweak or overhaul our practices, we develop an understanding of how the opportunities we provide students lead to increased learning.

> **Literacy walks provide opportunities for teachers, instructional coaches, and administrators to work together to support the growth of individual teachers, grade-level teachers, and the whole faculty.**

What a Literacy Walk Is Not

Literacy walks are not evaluations. They are not designed to judge or determine the effectiveness of a teacher or her practices. They *are* designed to collect information that teachers and administrators can discuss and learn from to grow together (Brockett & Hiemstra, 2018). They are also designed to collect data in a classroom about what teachers and students are doing that encourages learning.

Literacy walks are about learning. They should be designed to provide information for rich conversations among staff members to help student learning grow.

Literacy Walks Are	Literacy Walks Are Not
• Learning opportunities for teachers and administrators	• Evaluations of teachers by administrators
• Time to gather qualitative data about students' actions in response to instruction	• Time to judge students' actions in response to instruction
• Collegial, developmental, and school-based experiences for growth	• Evaluations or judgments of teachers by other teachers and colleagues
• Occasions to reflect on practice in teams	• Occasions for one-size-fits-all professional development
• Experiences that help to determine next-step actions and needs	• Experiences that don't lead to reflection or cause feelings of anxiousness
• In-context professional learning	• Out-of-context professional learning

WHY CONDUCT LITERACY WALKS?

Conduct literacy walks to:

- Help teachers and staff members learn from one another.
- Understand what teachers are doing and how what they are doing affects student learning.
- Learn about how different teachers implement the same lesson.
- See best practices in action.

Let me say this clearly: *Literacy walks are about teachers learning to improve their teaching and to improve student learning.* Administrators learn, too, during literacy walks. They learn what teachers need to do to get better at their own learning. They learn how to support their teachers and students.

Both teachers and administrators improve their practices when they (1) reflect and (2) learn from their reflections. Teachers have the power to get better by engaging in focused conversations about what they see students doing because of how they teach. Administrators can make better schoolwide and district-wide decisions based on the qualitative data they gather in classrooms during the walk.

Who Literacy Walks Are For

The purpose of literacy walks is to learn about literacy learning—the development of processes and skills related to reading, writing, and thinking—of students, in any content area and at any grade level. That means creating practices that help us notice and address the complicated layers of race, ethnicity, class, gender, learning style, etc., of each and all of our students. Students of color in particular have been historically underserved, which means, too often, their educational needs are not met over time (Fergus, 2016). We need to ensure students of color excel in literacy (Husband & Kang, 2020). We need to ensure students receiving special services do, too. We need to ensure that we guide students to read and write well, regardless of who they are and where they come from. Literacy walks enable us to examine our practices and work to ensure we're making our instruction and learning environments as equitable as possible.

What We Collect on a Literacy Walk

I have walked hundreds of classrooms in my more than 30 years as an educator. And during each walk, I've learned something important about the classroom I visit, primarily by taking notes and collecting the qualitative data I need to tell a story. The data might include observations of students or discussions with them about what they are learning—anything that helps us create a picture in our mind of what is happening. Here is what qualitative data may look like in an observation of small-group instruction:

> Sonia is sitting at the reading table with six students. To her left are sound cards (cards with an alphabet letter and a picture of an object or animal that begins with the letter's sound) attached to a whiteboard by magnets. She pronounces each sound and points to the letter and the picture. She says, "The word hay has the long-a sound," and asks students to say hay. Four out of six students say the word. Sonia repeats the sequence, but this time calls on students one by one. She smiles as each student says the word and gives an encouraging nod to the two students who had not said the word previously.

The note captures what Sonia is doing with her students and the environment she has created (a small group of students at the table, working with sounds). Although it may seem like a simple observation, this qualitative data helps me reflect on what I saw Sonia do when I was in her classroom. When you visit classrooms on a literacy walk, you will likely collect several pages of notes that will help you reflect on what you saw the students and teachers doing, and think about the teaching and learning environments and opportunities.

There are various ways to collect qualitative data during literacy walks, including note-taking and using checklists, as explained in Chapter 4. The key to a successful literacy walk is collecting data that paints a clear picture of what is happening in classrooms as it relates to teaching and learning. Detailed pictures are best. Data-Collection Tools should be augmented with notes in order to paint those pictures.

Because being observed by colleagues can be stressful, it's important to walk often enough that learning from one another becomes part of the school culture. I recently worked with a school that decided to implement literacy walks when they discovered that student comprehension was declining as students moved up grade levels. At first, the teachers were very nervous. They said they were apprehensive and sat in the launch meeting with their arms crossed or turned away from each other. In the spring, after a full round of walks was conducted, the staff met to set a goal for the following year. The atmosphere in the room was jubilant. There was synergy between the grade levels, and what they were learning from each other about teaching comprehension. One teacher said, "At the beginning, I dreaded the literacy walk day. Now, while I still get nervous about being observed, I look forward to the debrief with my colleagues."

How Literacy Walks Can Transform Your Classroom and School

When we walk one another's classrooms, we can learn together. We can see what learning looks like and we can determine what we need to do to better meet the needs of all our students. It is so easy to get caught up in what we *want* to do that we may lose sight of what we are actually doing during instruction. By taking notes during literacy walks, and reflecting on what we *intend, want,* and *do,* we can more closely align our instruction with student learning, which is transformative for our students and for us as educators.

I am so much more committed to a new way of teaching when I have been involved in the decision-making process, or when I truly understand why I need to make the change. The same is probably true for you.

> Literacy walks provide opportunities for teachers to deepen their practice by observing, listening to, and learning from colleagues.... Learning from others is powerful.

TRANSFORMING YOUR CLASSROOM

Claudia asked me for a coaching session after a series of literacy walks at her school. She shared that she saw things her colleagues were doing during their read-alouds that she thought were helpful in engaging student learning. I asked her to explain, and she told me they were not just reading aloud, but also stopping now and again to engage students in conversations about the book. I smiled and told her that the teachers were doing interactive read-alouds. Claudia had not heard of interactive read-alouds, so she and I planned her first attempt using the current novel she was reading to her class.

Literacy walks provide opportunities for teachers to deepen their practice by observing, listening to, and learning from colleagues, as Claudia did. Learning from others is powerful. In 1984, Malcolm Shepherd Knowles introduced the idea of *andragogy,* the art and science of adult learning, espousing four powerful principles that relate to literacy walks:

1. Adults need to be involved in the planning and evaluation of their instruction.

2. Experience (including mistakes) provides the basis for the learning activities.

3. Adults are most interested in learning subjects that have immediate relevance and impact to their job or personal life.

4. Adult learning is problem-centered rather than content-oriented (Kearsley, 2010; Knowles, 1984).

As a result of her literacy walk, Claudia focused on learning about read-alouds. But she did more than simply attend a professional development session on the topic. She watched expert read-alouds in action, thought about what she saw, and applied it to her own teaching, using me as a sounding board. She chose to work on interactive read-alouds as a personal-growth target. Our classroom environment, classroom culture, and signature practices can and will change as we learn together.

Literacy walks provide an opportunity for us to help a colleague meet a particular challenge she might be experiencing in her classroom. By observing, note-taking, and reflecting on our observations, we can help her overcome that challenge. As suggested in Knowles's adult-learning principles, problem-solving helps us reflect on our teaching, note what may or may not be happening with our students, and turn to our colleagues for solutions. No one has all the answers, all of the time. But working with colleagues brings us closer to answers (Brockett, 1994).

Too often, teachers get caught up in what Brené Brown calls perfect thinking (2010), feeling that they have to teach well all the time, and improve student learning all the time. The truth is that our instruction isn't *always* great. Students don't learn *all* of the time. But observation and reflection help us grow professionally and increase our efficacy (Bandura, 1977). Literacy walks provide space for observation and reflection—time to slow down to examine our practices.

TRANSFORMING YOUR SCHOOL

I was working with Sandra, Rochelle, and Mike to figure out how to help three fourth-grade students learn to segment words. In the past, the three teachers barely talked to one another, and two of them disagreed vehemently about the best way to teach students to read. And they were not alone. Many of the other teachers at the school were "meh" about collaborating during staff meetings. Collaboration was not part of the school culture.

Over time, as I worked with the teachers, they began to disagree constructively and offer solutions, including Sandra, Rochelle, and Mike, who had recently walked each other's classrooms during small-group instruction time. Sandra shared at a meeting that she noticed the students segmenting words rather effortlessly when Mike taught his lesson, but that her students were struggling to do it. I told Sandra that I thought it was great she was learning from watching Mike. I asked the group to reflect on how segmenting words connected to the school's goal of increasing the amount of time students read independently each day. Rochelle said that if students know how to segment words, they will be less frustrated while reading independently and be more likely to spend at least 20 minutes a day reading. Because of the literacy walks, the teachers were working together in a way that was collaborative, breaking down the walls of protection and being vulnerable and more authentic with each other and themselves. They were more willing to collaborate to solve problems of practice. The atmosphere of the school had changed from tense and siloed to hopeful and collegial.

What makes literacy walks transformational is the qualitative data you gather and then use during collective, collegial conversations with teammates. It is important to look at what the data shows to see what is really happening (Fritz, 1999). It's one thing to describe your teaching to your colleagues and another to invite them to observe and see your teaching firsthand. Without meaning to, we might describe our own teaching as we intend to implement it rather than how it actually plays out. Literacy walks can transform your

The Literacy Walk Process

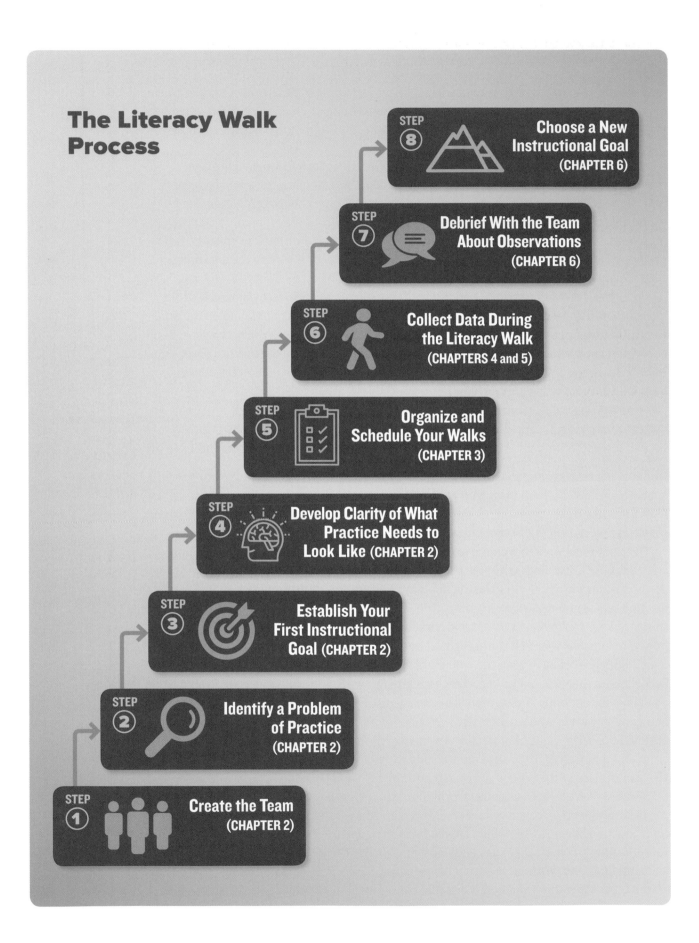

STEP 8 Choose a New Instructional Goal (CHAPTER 6)

STEP 7 Debrief With the Team About Observations (CHAPTER 6)

STEP 6 Collect Data During the Literacy Walk (CHAPTERS 4 and 5)

STEP 5 Organize and Schedule Your Walks (CHAPTER 3)

STEP 4 Develop Clarity of What Practice Needs to Look Like (CHAPTER 2)

STEP 3 Establish Your First Instructional Goal (CHAPTER 2)

STEP 2 Identify a Problem of Practice (CHAPTER 2)

STEP 1 Create the Team (CHAPTER 2)

work because you are focused on asking questions together and seeking answers to those questions. You are developing understanding by walking each other's classrooms and noting what is happening, how students are working and interacting, and how the teacher is setting up learning and responding to students.

When we, as teachers and administrators, invest in solving problems of practice collectively, we authentically work through our thinking and questions. We focus more systematically and strategically on implementing literacy practices that lead to student learning. Whether we are part of a team of two or ten, literacy walks help us engage in productive inquiry and take collective responsibility for student learning (Mierink, Imants, Mejier, & Verloop, 2010). They are a way of understanding the current realities of your school. Taking them is like holding a mirror up to the organization.

Bringing It All Together

Literacy walks work best with a systematic approach. In Chapters 2 through 6, I describe the series of steps on the previous page—a process that helps a team get organized and stay on track, gives purpose to the walk, and supports you in reaching short- and long-range goals for learning. You'll find data-gathering tools and directions for using them in Chapters 4 and 5. By learning how to use the tools, you and the team will transform how you learn together, and how you gather and use data for collegial conversations to learn together. Literacy walks are powerful for helping you to understand what instructional practices are working best, and what might need to be adapted or changed.

What makes literacy walks transformational is the qualitative data you gather and then use during collective, collegial conversations with teammates.

CHAPTER 2

Getting Started
Develop Schoolwide Goals for Learning

"I introduced the idea of literacy walks to my staff because I wanted them to be in charge of their own professional growth based on school data. It was powerful for all of us. I learned to support the teachers based on what they identified as needs."

—MICHAEL, ELEMENTARY PRINCIPAL

By doing literacy walks with your colleagues, you are, in essence, focusing on a problem to be solved—specifically, a "problem of practice" that helps you learn and continuously improve (Horn & Little, 2010). You and your colleagues build a culture of collaboration by working together to focus on practices that will make meaningful changes in day-to-day instruction— changes that keep your school vibrant and alive because you are continually looking at student learning. You are considering how you can help students become strong readers and writers, and adjusting what and how you teach to make that happen (Fullan & Quinn, 2016).

In this chapter, I explain the first four steps of literacy walks:

1. **Create the Team**
2. **Identify a Problem of Practice**
3. **Establish Your First Instructional Goal**
4. **Develop Clarity of What Practice Needs to Look Like**
5. Organize and Schedule Your Walks
6. Collect Data During the Literacy Walk
7. Debrief With the Team About Observations
8. Choose a New Instructional Goal

Step 1: Create the Team

To give teachers agency in setting their own goals, and to help create the conditions for implementing change in literacy practices schoolwide, teams should be made up of teachers and administrators, teachers and coaches, or teachers who are coaching one another. From time to time, teams may be made up only of school or district administrators. However, it's best when fellow teachers are part of the team because the goal is for teachers, instructional coaches, and administrators to work together to support teacher growth and the growth of school organizations (Taylor & Chanter, 2019).

It's important to develop trust amongst all the staff members so they are confident that the team is collecting data for the purpose of making change, and not simply evaluating practice. One way to develop trust is by copying your observational notes and distributing them, or by putting them in a virtual shared document such as a Google Doc. (See Chapter 4 for information on taking observational notes.) A small team may need to conduct the walks over a few days in order to visit all the classrooms, following the same protocol that I discussed earlier, spending 15 to 20 minutes in each classroom and recording its observations. Once the team has gathered and interpreted their observations, the results can be shared transparently with the entire staff. (See the next chapter for details on sharing data.)

At the start, select a team facilitator to keep the process on track. The team facilitator need not be the principal. You might consider a teacher. Use the opportunity for equitable leadership development and power sharing. The facilitator schedules the literacy walks, sends emails to remind everyone of the literacy walk date and schedule, and leads the debrief meetings held after the walks.

Step 2: Identify a Problem of Practice

By following the continuous learning cycle in the chart below, your team can collaboratively choose a focus and work at it together (Hall & Hord, 2019). The cycle provides a foundation for the literacy walk process.

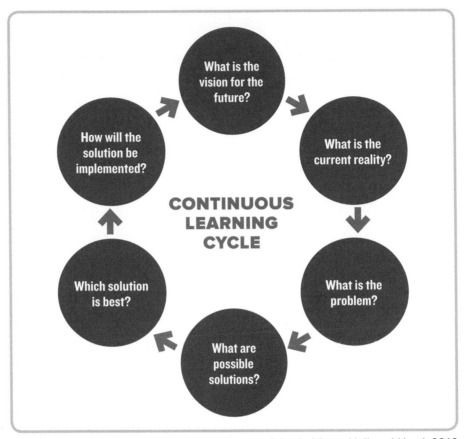

Adapted from Hall and Hord, 2019

With the cycle in mind, start by considering current reality at the school. Look at practices in place in most classrooms, and identify ones that could be improved. Student data can help. Then, moving through the cycle, identify a problem of practice (Horn & Little, 2010), a specific challenge related to student learning. For instance, if data indicates that many students are not reading fluently by third grade, the problem of practice might be focusing on how to improve fluency in the earlier grades. If students are struggling to articulate their thinking about what they have read, and capturing their thoughts in writing, the problem of practice might be discovering how to engage students in powerful lessons to help them think deeper and write about their thinking. Whatever the problem of practice, base it on student data. As you continue to move through the cycle, consider possible solutions and what they would look like in practice. Brainstorm with the team what teaching and learning would look like if those solutions were applied. Following the continuous learning cycle prepares you to walk classrooms and collect data.

Take a look at the qualitative data below that staff members at Redmond Elementary School compiled following a literacy walk in which they focused on student engagement and talk during shared reading. Their findings led them to ask themselves: Why are students staying on the surface of the texts, and what might motivate them to engage and go deeper?

LITERACY WALK
REDMOND ELEMENTARY

Team-Identified Problem of Practice: Students are not engaged during shared reading and, therefore, are not developing comprehension skills or oral language.

STEPS AGREED UPON TO SOLVE THE PROBLEM OF PRACTICE	
Teachers have a time dedicated to shared reading.	Teachers in 12 out of 12 classrooms were doing shared reading.
Teachers were stopping periodically and asking questions about text and encouraging students to respond by discussing the text.	• All teachers (12/12) were stopping periodically to ask questions. • In 8/12 classrooms, the students were able to answer simple questions like *who, what, why, when,* and *where.* • In 4/12 classrooms, the students were able to ask questions of the text themselves. • In 2/12 classrooms, the students referred back to the text to answer their own questions.
Teachers posed questions to help students make predictions about what will happen next in the story, based on details and prior knowledge of the text.	• All teachers (12/12) were stopping at points in the text to model making predictions. All teachers did this at least once. • Students did not make the predictions the teachers modeled, and the students agreed with or added on to the prediction.
Teachers guided students to think through earlier predictions and why they did or did not come true, referring to the text for details.	• All teachers (12/12) were modeling how to stop and check the text in order to think through their predictions. • 10/12 teachers did a think-aloud during their modeling, slowing down and really talking about what they were thinking. • Students were listening.

Group thoughts following the literacy walk:

- As a school, we have a dedicated time for shared reading.
- We are doing a lot of modeling but not allowing time for students to do the thinking after the teacher models.
- Our students can answer surface-level questions about the text.
- Sometimes our students can think about the text and ask questions, but this happens only when the teacher slows down and provides a lot of wait time for the students.
- We all need to work to allow students time to do the thinking and talking.

Once literacy walks become a regular part of your school's culture, they will provide a data stream that you can use to establish goals.

Teachers noted that they did not feel confident teaching shared reading and incorporating writing into shared reading. They were confident reading aloud as students followed along, but, during and after the reading found themselves resorting mostly to *who, what, why, when,* and *where* questions. The teachers also noted that when they asked those surface-level questions, students often didn't respond. So, the Redmond team settled on a problem of practice using think-alouds to improve teachers' shared reading practices and deepen students' engagement.

The problem of practice the staff members at Sunshine Elementary School decided on also related to helping students think more deeply about text. Based on results of their chosen comprehensive assessment results from the previous year, the teachers determined that students were fluent in decoding words, but were largely unable to answer the comprehension questions that required deeper thinking. See a summary of the data on the next page.

By looking at your data, you can get a clear idea of a problem of practice that you need to focus on. Once literacy walks become a regular part of your school's culture, they will provide a data stream that you can use to establish goals. Until then, however, your staff will need to rely on other data streams, such as:

- Running records
- School benchmark data for reading and writing
- Observational records
- Published literacy assessment such as Beaver's *Developmental Reading Assessment,* Richardson and Walther's *Next Step Guided Reading Assessment,* or Fountas and Pinnell's *Benchmark Assessment Systems*
- State or district assessments

SUNSHINE ELEMENTARY STUDENT DATA

Grade Level:	Teachers:		Year:
Third	Funton, Marks, Hernandez, Tovar		2021–2022

LAFT READING COMP TEST

	LAFT 1	LAFT 2	LAFT 3	LAFT 4
% Proficient Comprehension	39%	54%	59%	69%

READING ASSESSMENT

Scores Overall	First Quarter				Second Quarter				Third Quarter				Fourth Quarter			
	Date	Stage	Level	Decode words	Date	Stage	Level	Decode words	Date	Stage	Level	Decode words	Date	Stage	Level	Decode words
	10/21	Majority are emergent readers.	G–I	85%	12/21	Majority are emergent readers.	H–J	87%	3/22	Majority are early readers.	I–J	91%	5/22	Majority are early readers.	K–M	92%

Anecdotal Notes

Most students were at the early reading stage at the beginning of third grade and did not make progress rapidly. Many students could not answer comprehension questions as part of a running record, and scored a 2 out of 5 on the rubric we used for comprehension during the first and second quarters. However, they scored higher in decoding.

Step 3: Establish Your First Instructional Goal

When establishing a goal for your team to work on together, don't look for a quick fix to a problem of practice because it will prove disappointing and possibly lead to unintended consequences (Stroh & Zurcher, 2020). I have seen that happen. For example, at Pembroke Elementary School, where I was working recently, spring DRA scores indicated that 76 percent of the third graders were not reading within grade-level range. So the team decided to increase the number of minutes each child spent in small-group reading each day. At first, that seemed like a wise goal. All the teachers had been trained in small-group reading, so they felt confident achieving it. In the beginning, things seemed to be going well. But over time, the teachers realized the students weren't making the gains they had hoped for.

Because of their established goal, the team used the literacy walks to look at minutes spent in small-group reading. They were not looking at ways in which each teacher was being responsive to students' reading needs. As such, teachers began to question the goal because it did not allow them to make professional decisions on the amount of time each student needed in small-group reading. They wanted to modify the amount of time based on each student's particular strengths and challenges. They wanted the goal to be more about meeting students' needs in small-group reading and less about time spent in small-group reading.

Though the goal seemed like an obvious choice at first, ultimately the teachers felt let down. That is why I caution you to look deeply when establishing your goal and thinking about your practice. Later, the team established a new goal—to allow teachers to decide the amount of time each child spent in small-group reading, based on his or her needs and rate of progress. The Pembroke team continued to focus on providing small-group reading to each student; however, it stopped focusing on minutes and started focusing on needs.

PERFORMANCE GOALS VS. LEARNING GOALS

The mistake that the Pembroke team made was to focus on a *performance* goal, when it should've been focusing on a *learning* goal. A performance goal helps you validate your ability to do something (Brown, Roediger & McDaniel, 2014). For the Pembroke team, that was minutes spent in small-group reading. A *learning* goal helps you develop instructional practices and reflect on your efforts. Kaplan and Maehr (2007) define it as "a purpose of personal development and growth that guides achievement-related behavior and task-engagement" (p. 151). When your team is working together on implementing highly effective literacy practices, focus on learning about the impact of your efforts.

DEVELOPING A TEAM GOAL

Once you have gathered your data, have a conversation as a team to develop a goal, which will help members maintain focus during the literacy walks so that they know what they are looking for. It can be intimidating for a teacher if she feels classroom visitors are checking out all things going on! With an agreed-upon goal, everyone knows the focus of the walk—and the teacher's fears are more likely to be allayed.

Brainstorming With the Team

Developing a goal requires brainstorming with your team and listening to all ideas, following a set of rules that all members agree to, such as:

- Setting a time limit for brainstorming.
- Considering all ideas and placing them on a list.
- Making no value judgments.

Working effectively with a team is about inclusivity. When you collectively gather evidence of literacy practices you see being implemented, and analyze the results together, you make room for multiple voices, perspectives, and viewpoints. By working together you grow together. Goals set by one person are usually short-sighted, and staff members probably won't get behind it. Also, setting goals in a vacuum can lead to misunderstanding among staff members at best and resentment at worst.

Inclusivity means all voices are heard and honored. For that to happen, more outspoken team members may need to hold back occasionally so that quieter members can share thoughts and ideas.

It is helpful for the facilitator to have a few strategies in mind to ensure productive and efficient conversations. After all, so little time is available for teachers, administrators, and support staff to get together in one space. You will want the time you do have to be as productive as possible. Strategies such as intervening to keep the discussion flowing and welcoming to all participants can help (Eller, 2004). The team facilitator may implement some of the following actions to help the discussion go well.

1. Set norms for conversations. At your first meeting, discuss norms that the participants would like to follow. As participants offer them, write them down and post them so they are visible during the entire meeting. Here are some possible norms:

- Enjoy yourself and have fun.
- Use *I* statements.
- Listen carefully and make space for multiple points of view.
- When participants state something in the negative, ask them to reframe in a strengths-based way.
- If you feel slighted, state your feelings, using *I* statements.
- If you feel you have slighted someone, make amends.

2. Invite, don't tell. Inviting participants to focus on a process or task in the meeting, rather than telling them to, is likely to be more effective (Bens, 2005). If that's not the case for a particular member, check with that member individually to see if you can remove any roadblock that is preventing her or him from fully participating in the discussion.

Sometimes people may not trust the group or may feel vulnerable. Listen to the person before attempting to re-invite him or her to participate or diverting him or her to another activity.

3. Seek everyone's input. When one person is dominating the discussion, turn to others for input. Thank the person who is dominating and say something like, "So we can hear all voices in the room, let's move to someone else for input and ideas." Then call on another person.

4. Diffuse heightening emotions. If disagreements begin turning into arguments, and participants are no longer hearing each other, bring the emotion back to a more normal level by making a clarifying statement. You might reflect on what you are hearing, and then move the conversation to another point. For example, you may say, "I can see that we are not agreeing with each other. This is what I am hearing from Sara.… José, this is what I think you are expressing.… Now that we have discussed that, let's move on to another point."

5. Remain on point and topic. Sometimes the conversation will get off track. Participants will lose sight of a point being made and start talking about a different point, or they will bring up a past topic and lose focus on the current one. When that happens, recognize that the conversation is off track and reframe the point or topic.

6. Minimize "Yes, but…" statements. When participants feel that ideas being presented will not work, they'll sometimes shut down those ideas, rather than letting them flow. A sign that this is happening is when participants begin statements with, "Yes, but…" Of course, the occasional "Yes, but…" statement is normal and helpful, but don't let them get out of hand. Redirect positively by saying something like, "I am hearing a lot of 'Yes, but…' statements in our conversation. Rather than thinking about how ideas *won't* work, let's be more creative in our brainstorming, problem solving, and idea generating. If you feel compelled to offer a 'Yes, but' statement, don't just identify the problem with the idea. Offer a solution."

CREATING PATHWAYS THROUGH CONFLICTS

Communicating with some team members may be difficult. Some members may contribute too much, others may not contribute at all. By establishing team norms and processes, you ensure that everyone's voice is heard and valued. Discuss and set team norms and processes before embarking on literacy walks.

Step 4: Develop Clarity of What Practice Needs to Look Like

In his research, John Hattie (2008) showed that teacher clarity has great impact on student learning. That means the clearer a teacher is in describing the objectives for a lesson, and remaining loyal to those objectives in her instruction, the greater the student learning. That is true for adult learners as well. If you are going to work well together as a team, you need to be as clear as possible with one another.

A problem that occurs sometimes, however, is that we are not always clear in our objectives when we write lessons collaboratively; we don't always *see* the learning outcome. That is why when I do professional development on small-group reading instruction, I am careful to describe what I mean early on about it because if there are 20 people in my session, there could be 20 different ideas about what the instruction should look like.

For instance, when I explained Redmond School's choice to focus on shared reading, you probably thought about what you know about shared reading. That is great! But if you were part of a team about to embark on literacy walks, ideally, you and your fellow team members would talk about *how* you do shared reading. We cannot make assumptions about each other's practices. Developing clarity is not about coming up with the one right way to do something. It's about having a collective understanding of instructional practices, what those practices look like in action, and how observing and reflecting on them will help you reach your goal (Elmore & City, 2007).

Developing clarity is often the step that's skipped because people make assumptions about each other's understanding. Listen to your teammates and ask questions such as, "What does this practice mean to you? How would you implement it?" Clarity is essential to arriving at shared understanding. It is also essential to helping one another improve your literacy practices (City, Elmore, Fiarman & Teitel, 2009).

The chart at right contains notes from a meeting at the Sunshine School at which team members focused on clarifying their goal. You can see that they defined what they meant by "encourage student thinking about their reading" and listed ideas for achieving that.

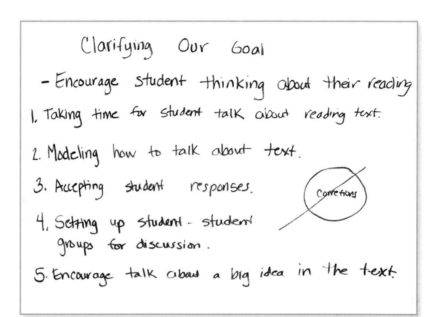

Clarifying Our Goal
- Encourage student thinking about their reading
1. Taking time for student talk about reading text.
2. Modeling how to talk about text.
3. Accepting student responses.
4. Setting up student - student groups for discussion.
5. Encourage talk about a big idea in the text.

~~Corrections~~

Bringing It All Together

Once you begin literacy walks, you will gather information from your classrooms that will help you learn and grow as a team. As you learn and grow, you'll adjust your literacy practices to help students learn to read, write, and think more deeply. You will engage in continuous learning by looking at data and information you gather during literacy walks, and then choose a new goal or refine an existing goal and continue the work (Bryk, Gomez, Grunow & LeMathieu, 2015).

CHAPTER 3

Walking Together
Organize and Schedule

"Learning about our school and our students' learning with my team opened my eyes as to what students can really do for themselves. I am so thrilled to see the ways they work with texts."

—JOHNIKA, FOURTH-GRADE TEACHER

I have been told that literacy walks are simultaneously exhilarating and challenging. Working with a team may ask us to exercise different muscles and take time and practice to establish a rhythm. When we collaborate with peers, we are more likely to see the changes we need to make in our instruction. And as we set and commit to new goals together, we are more likely to implement changes and reach those goals.

In this chapter, I look at what happens during the literacy walks to help you better understand their elements. Specifically, I look at structures and schedules of walking classrooms.

Literacy walks are about learning. By visiting classrooms with your team and gathering information about what is happening there, you learn about literacy practices firsthand and how they are affecting student learning (Boel & Farizio, 2013). You come to understand what teaching and learning look like at your school as you look at the work on the walls and students' desks. As you check out the tasks students are involved in, pay close attention to instruction and also student-to-student interactions, teacher-to-student interactions, student-to-teacher interactions, and the level of conversation about reading and writing.

I explained the first four steps to the literacy walks in Chapter 2. In this chapter, let's look at the fifth step:

1. Create the Team
2. Identify a Problem of Practice
3. Establish Your First Instructional Goal
4. Develop Clarity of What Practice Needs to Look Like
5. **Organize and Schedule Your Walks**
6. Collect Data During the Literacy Walk
7. Debrief With the Team About Observations
8. Choose a New Instructional Goal

Step 5: Organize and Schedule Your Walks

There are multiple ways to organize and schedule literacy walks. Depending on the size and makeup of the team, all members can walk together or break into small groups. Be sure to arrange for substitutes for teachers on the team. The examples below are designed to give you ideas for organizing and scheduling your walks.

WALKING AS A TEAM, WITH TEACHERS ROTATING BETWEEN TEACHING AND OBSERVING

In this example, teachers, administrators, coaches, and support staff walk together, with each teacher on the team replacing the substitute when the team arrives at her classroom. For example, a group of four teachers at one or two grade levels will start with four subs covering their classes while they meet to launch the walks. Then one teacher will go back to his classroom to teach and the remaining members of the team will come to watch him teach. The four teachers will rotate so that each has a chance to teach and be observed by the others. The substitute steps aside and the teacher on the team takes over. When the walk in her room is finished, the sub steps back in and the teacher resumes walking with the team.

EXAMPLE 1

If you have one team with four teachers at the same grade level, visit each classroom and have each teacher replace the substitute when you arrive. Continue the rotation until four teachers have been observed.

Round 1	8:30–8:50	Room 13
Round 2	8:50–9:10	Room 15
Round 3	9:10–9:30	Room 20
Round 4	9:30–9:50	Room 22

WALKING AS A TEAM, WITH TEACHERS ONLY OBSERVING

In this example, teachers on the team, as well as administrators, coaches, and support staff, observe teachers at grade levels other than their own. A group of first- and second-grade teachers, for example, might walk the classrooms of third-, fourth-, and fifth-grade teachers. As such, a substitute will be needed for each teacher on the team for the duration of the entire walk.

EXAMPLE 2

If you have two teams walking at the same time, create a schedule that spells out when each team will visit each classroom, as in the example below. You can cover multiple classrooms with a team visiting each classroom once, or fewer classrooms with each team visiting the same classroom twice.

Round 1	8:30–8:50	Team A: Room 13	Team B: Room 15
Round 2	8:50–9:10	Team A: Room 15	Team B: Room 13
Round 3	9:10–9:30	Team A: Room 20	Team B: Room 22
Round 4	9:30–9:50	Team A: Room 22	Team B: Room 20

EXAMPLE 3

If you have three teams walking at the same time, create a schedule that spells out when each team will visit each classroom, as in the example below. By following this example, you may be able to cover the whole school, with teachers visiting within their grade levels or across grade levels.

Round 1	8:30–8:50	Team A: Room 1	Team B: Room 2	Team C: Room 3
Round 2	8:50–9:10	Team A: Room 4	Team B: Room 5	Team C: Room 6
Round 3	9:10–9:30	Team A: Room 7	Team B: Room 8	Team C: Room 9
Round 4	9:30–9:50	Team A: Room 10	Team B: Room 11	Team C: Room 12
Round 5	9:50–10:10	Team A: Room 13	Team B: Room 14	Team C: Room 15

Bringing It All Together

Whether or not your school has the funds to pay for substitutes to support the literacy walks, your team can embark on walks and plan a schedule that fits the needs of the team and the school. Literacy walks are about observing each other teach. I have provided a couple of examples in this chapter of how the schedule might look, but you might brainstorm a schedule and format that works best for your school. Don't allow lack of funds for substitutes to get in the way. I have seen schools where the administrators gladly covered classes so teachers could walk together. Be creative in figuring out the best solution and schedule!

PART II
DURING THE WALK

Learning from Literacy Walks

CHAPTER 4

Taking Note
Reflect on Teaching and Learning During the Literacy Walks

"When literacy walks first started at my school, I felt intimidated because people were taking notes. I wanted to know what they were writing down about my teaching. Once it was my turn to go on a literacy walk, I realized the notes were to help us remember what we saw, not to judge. I felt so much better about the process."

—ROBERT, SEVENTH-GRADE TEACHER

Taking notes on the literacy walks helps you understand the current state of instruction at the school (Stake, 2005). The team comes together after the literacy walk, using information in the notes, to develop a picture of what's working and what isn't. This is qualitative analysis of data, not judgment (Curtis & City, 2009).

Christopher, a third-grade teacher, was excited to join his team for literacy walks. It would be a new opportunity for him. He listened eagerly to what the facilitator was saying as she set up his team to walk each other's classrooms. Then she passed out note-taking sheets. Christopher noticed that they would be required to write down things they saw in the classrooms in relation to the school's focus. He suddenly felt nervous. He was afraid his colleagues would be judgmental, and he imagined all the disparaging comments they might record about his teaching. But the facilitator reassured the team. "This process is not about judging one another. It is about collecting objective data to get a snapshot of what is going on at the school today," she explained. Relieved, Christopher could now see that the notes could help him evaluate what his students learned from his teaching.

Literacy walks are about the school community working together to increase students' ability to read, write, and think. As a result, all members of a community—staff, students, and parents—benefit. Build trusting, accountable relationships. Some teachers may fear that the notes are going to be used against them in some way, or to evaluate them. If trust is broken because of judgmental notes, the learning process that happens during literacy walks will break down, and your team will lose its power to lead its own learning. In this chapter, I discuss the sixth step in the process:

1. Create the Team
2. Identify a Problem of Practice
3. Establish Your First Instructional Goal
4. Develop Clarity of What Practice Needs to Look Like
5. Organize and Schedule Your Walks
6. **Collect Data During the Literacy Walk**
7. Debrief With the Team About Observations
8. Choose a New Instructional Goal

Step 6: Collect Data During the Literacy Walk

There are a variety of ways to collect data during the literacy walks. You can take literal notes and descriptive notes, for example, or fill out checklists—and by that, I mean checklists *with notes*. Notes bring meaning to what you observe. They help you understand the culture of classrooms by providing data that you work with in the debrief meetings (Bernhardt, 2017). Notes should be as objective and detailed as possible to develop *understanding*.

LITERAL NOTES

When you take literal notes, you write down exactly what you see happening in the classroom, with no conjecture or opinion. (Saphier, Haley-Speca & Gower, 2008). You do not summarize what you are seeing. So, for instance, you would not write, "Twenty students were listening to the teacher read aloud. Eight students were very interested and twelve students seemed uninterested."

Example of literal notes

Instead, you would write something like, "Twenty students were listening to the teacher read aloud. Eight students were facing the teacher. Six students were gazing at the ceiling, three students had their heads down and eyes closed, and three were doing other work in a notebook." It's helpful to date and time-stamp literal notes, especially if you're walking over several days and/or visiting several classrooms.

CHECKLISTS

Checklists can help you capture and quantify the data you collect during literacy walks (Stake, 1995). So, perhaps you walked many classrooms in one day, but won't be meeting with the entire team to debrief right away. You can use a checklist to capture your data into meaningful snapshots of what you observed that can later be unpacked when you meet to debrief.

Note how the data is tabulated in the checklist on the next page. A pair of teachers walked the classrooms because resources didn't allow for substitutes for more than two teachers at a time. They conducted walks over three days, following the protocol described in Chapter 3. They spent no more than 20 minutes in each classroom, taking descriptive notes. After completing all the walks, the two teachers reviewed the notes and highlighted salient points, created a checklist with tabulations based on those notes, and shared the checklist with the larger team, which allowed members to process the data quickly and easily.

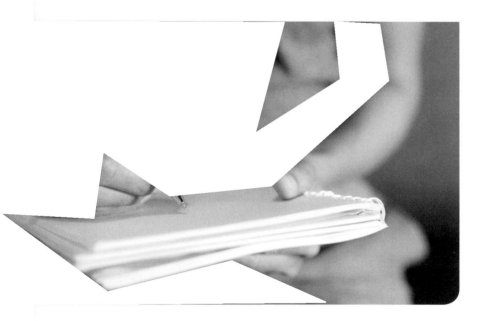

FOCUS	TABULATION: Number of classrooms where the practice or behavior was observed
Environment	
☑ Complex and engaging text is used for shared reading (texts have multiple levels of meaning appropriate for the grade level, there are complex and/or multiple themes, and language is not too simplified).	15
☐ Two to four books are read aloud daily.	Unknown
☑ There is a classroom library that is large and extensive in topics, text types, and genres.	20 — three classrooms belong to new teachers, so library is developing
☑ Classroom is filled with books/texts on a variety of topics, and genres and books/texts reflect students' race, culture, and identities, and those of others.	19
Comprehension	
☐ Recognize major differences between genres and genre features.	Not observed
☑ Ask and answer questions about the text.	15
☑ Note the illustrations and the meaning illustrations provide to the text.	20
☑ Retell the story including key details and discuss the central message or theme of the story.	20
☑ Make predictions about what will happen next in the story based on details.	12
☑ Use illustrations and details to describe characters, setting, and events.	17

This checklist contains data that was collected from several classrooms based on the school's problem of practice.

A CHECKLIST CHECK-IN

Be careful with checklists. While they are an efficient way to collect data quickly, literacy walks can devolve into simply determining if a particular practice was in place or not. Use checklists sparingly and focus more often on taking detailed notes.

I learned this while working with a school district a few years ago. At first, I recommended the teams use checklists to note quickly what they were seeing in classrooms. I wound up seeing two unexpected and disappointing results during the debrief:

1. The teachers felt judged because the checklists only captured if a practice was seen or not seen during the literacy walks. They did not capture rich descriptions of what teachers and students were doing. As such, during the debrief, the team did not have a clear picture of what had happened in the classrooms.

2. The debrief was very limited. Because there were no notes, the team could not discuss with insight what they thought students could do based on the instruction they were receiving. The team had trouble choosing a new goal to work on and could not make meaningful recommendations for professional development.

While I have cautioned against the use of checklists alone, I have also worked with teams that needed some direction when walking colleagues' classrooms because they were not certain about what to look for, and the checklists allowed for precision and confidence in their conversations. Your school might already use checklists, but remember what's important is to have rich, thoughtful notes, with or without a checklist—but not a checklist alone!

DESCRIPTIVE NOTES

With descriptive notes you write down facts, as you do with literal notes, but you add details about what you see, such as what you notice about the setting, behaviors, and conversations (Schwandt, 2015), as well as your thoughts, feelings, and impressions, without being judgmental. Be sure to reflect on what you see as constructively as possible.

In some ways, I find descriptive notes easier to take than literal notes because I'm not trying to write down almost everything that is happening. Instead, I'm observing, noticing, reflecting—and then writing.

The notes need to be as accurate as possible because you get only one chance to take them (Emerson, Fretz & Shaw, 2011). They also need to be rich in detail to give you truly useful information to think about in debrief meetings. Here is a descriptive iteration of the literal notes example on page 30: "Twenty students were listening to the teacher read aloud. The teacher's voice was monotone. Eight of the students were watching her as she read and were paying attention. They looked engaged. Twelve of the students were not engaged. About half of them were looking around the room, and the rest had their heads down on their desks or were writing in a notebook." If you notice, there are some descriptive words in the notes, such as *engaged* and *monotone*. But they are not judgments. They are backed up with observable details.

In essence, you want to paint a picture of what you are seeing. So, for example, if you notice during a walk that the reading corner looks comfortable, don't merely write, "The reading corner is comfortable." Instead, write something like, "The reading corner is comfortable, with its pillows and lamp for ambient lighting. The

> The notes need to be as accurate as possible. . . . They also need to be rich in detail to give you truly useful information to think about in debrief meetings.

Feb. 10   Cliff 2nd grade

T began word work lesson by writing 3 multisyllabic words on the board. He stated that the class was going to work on sounding out multisyllabic words so they could attack bigger words while reading.

Students were listening and most faced T. T explained how to break up first words. Students listened and then repeated after T.

Students caught on quickly and were able to sound out 3 additional words that T wrote on the board.

Example of descriptive notes

books are easy to access." You can also add speculations and interpretations of what you are observing (Emerson, Fretz & Shaw, 2011). For example, if you notice four students talking energetically about a book for an extended period, you might write, "The way the students worked together for the 10 minutes indicates that they have practiced how to talk together about books, and that they have ample time to talk together about books. No time was wasted."

Categorizing Observations in Descriptive Notes

When taking descriptive notes, it can help to organize your observations into categories—areas of focus to help you decide what to note and where to place your notes.

DESCRIPTIVE NOTES BY CATEGORY

Mullhouse 10/21

Environment	EVIDENCE	
Sound wall is in a place that can be used during instruction.	The classroom is set up with the sound wall near the carpet area. The children are on the carpet facing the sound wall. Teacher is modeling using the sound wall.	
Sound wall includes the sound cards from the current lesson.	The use of the sound wall was really helpful for students. They were making connections between sounds in words and the letters.	
Phonological Awareness	**TEACHER SAYS/DOES**	**STUDENTS SAY/DO**
Teacher taught how to count words in spoken sentences.	Teacher was modeling how to count words in the sentence that the class brainstormed together.	Students suggested sentences to the teacher and then helped the teacher count the words in the sentence.
Teacher taught how to count and pronounce phonemes in spoken words.	The teacher modeled how to count phonemes in a word.	Students counted the sounds that they heard in the words that the teacher said aloud.
Teacher modeled blending phonemes into spoken words.	Teacher identified three phonemes and then blended them to say a word. She told the students what she did and why.	Students suggested words to the teacher and then said each phoneme. Then they blended the sounds to say each word with the teacher.

In Chapter 5, you'll learn about the customized Data-Collection Tool, which provides space in the first column for you to capture "look-fors" (i.e., essential and observable elements of instruction) that best match your team goal. In the appendix, pages 100–140, and at scholastic.com/LiteracyWalksResources, you'll find Look-For Banks for each component of a comprehensive literacy program: read-aloud, shared reading, small-group and independent reading, writing, word work, and language.

The Data-Collection Tool's second and third columns provide space for you to write descriptive notes during your literacy walks. See the next page for an example of a tool created to capture descriptive notes on first-grade practices in foundational skills.

CURRENT-REALITY/DESIRED-FUTURE GAP ANALYSIS

Once you gather notes, you may want to analyze them to help the team take action. While I recommend that the team first go through the team debrief, it can be helpful to do a gap analysis either before or after the debrief. A gap analysis allows you to look at your team goal in relation to your notes, and identify what might be missing from practice. In other words, you look at the current reality and, based on your goal, desired future.

Start the gap analysis with a visioning exercise. Post the team goal, and ask participants to think about the following:

- What do you see happening in classrooms when you think about our team goal?
- What would classrooms look like and sound like if we were to reach that goal?

> A gap analysis allows you to look at your team goal in relation to your notes, and identify what might be missing from practice. In other words, you look at the current reality and, based on your goal, desired future.

FIRST-GRADE DATA-COLLECTION TOOL FOCUSING ON FOUNDATIONAL READING SKILLS

Data-Collection Tool

Team Goal:	To enable students to hear sounds in words, and to segment and manipulate sounds to make real and nonsense words		

Grade(s): 1	Teacher(s): **Osgood**	Date(s): 2/7

Component(s) to Observe:	☐ Read-Aloud ☐ Shared Reading ☐ Small-Group and Independent Reading
	☒ Word Work ☐ Writing ☐ Language

Classroom Arrangement:	☐ Whole-Class ☒ Small Group ☐ Individual

LOOK-FORS BY CATEGORY	TEACHER SAYS/DOES	STUDENTS SAY/DO
Phonological Awareness • Count and pronounce phonemes in spoken words. • Blend phonemes into spoken words. • Isolate and pronounce initial, medial, and final phonemes in single-syllable words. • Blend phonemes, including consonant blends, into spoken words. • Identify the number of words in spoken sentences. • Segment syllables in spoken words. • Change or extend simple single-syllable words by adding or substituting phonemes. **Phonics** • Decode (segment and blend) single-syllable words. • Decode (segment and blend) two-syllable words by breaking them into syllables.		

The Data-Collection Tool's second and third columns provide space for you to write descriptive notes during your literacy walks.

Steps of a Current-Reality/Desired-Future Gap Analysis

1. Revisit the team goal and discuss what classrooms would look and sound like if the goal was reached. On note paper, have team members write their thoughts individually.

2. On a chart labeled Current Reality, write down observations team members share from their checklists and notes—what they actually saw and experienced on the walk. They may share tabulated data from the checklist, but also anecdotal notes and memories to add detail.

3. On another chart labeled Desired Future, write down what team members share from their notes until you arrive at a rich, vibrant, mutually agreed-upon description of what classrooms might look and sound like.

4. On a third chart labeled Gap, posted in between the Current Reality chart and the Desired Future chart, write down what team members say are the causes of the gap between the current reality and desired future.

5. As a group, analyze the causes of the gap and decide on how to take steps to move toward the desired future, which may mean modifying the team goal.

(Fritz, 1999)

GAP

Goal: Increase student independent reading

- lack of classroom library books
- old, uninteresting books available for students
- no dedicated time in daily schedule
- only do book talks sporadically
- requiring students to test on each book read decreases reading motivation
- not sharing progress to goal during staff meetings

Bringing It All Together

As I've tried to make clear in this chapter, there are many ways to take notes during literacy walks. The method you choose is up to you and your team; just be sure everyone takes notes the same way to ensure consistency in your data, which will support a powerful and meaningful debrief meeting. Keep in mind that notes are just data, and data is just information. Without interpretation of information, nothing will be learned and nothing will change. By setting goals, observing practice closely, taking careful notes, and debriefing thoughtfully, together, you and other members of your team can improve teaching and learning opportunities for students.

CHAPTER 5

Digging Deeper
Create and Use the Data-Collection Tools

"I found that using a literacy walk tool with descriptive categories to be helpful for me and the teachers. We were more precise in what we wanted to see students doing because of the teaching. It brought clarity to our conversations."

—ESTELLE, LITERACY COACH

Thus far, I've discussed how to organize, lead, and participate in literacy walks, stressing the importance of teachers and administrators working as a team to learn about instruction and student learning. In Chapter 4, I explained how to take notes for dynamic team discussions. In this chapter, I dive deeper into that topic.

Learner-Facing Data-Collection Tools

The tools we use during literacy walks allow us to collect the data we need to inform our reflection and discussion. Learner-facing tools help us capture information about the students. They also help us capture information about the learning environment and classroom community, with an emphasis on the student, not the teacher.

When we focus on teaching, we focus on the adult—the teacher and what she or he is doing. When we focus on the student, we focus on his or her experience, feelings, and, of course, learning. Students are central to the literacy walk because they are central to the instruction (City, Elmore, Fiarman & Teitel, 2009). Focusing on them compels us to look closely at and for instructional outcomes.

THE NUTS AND BOLTS OF THE DATA-COLLECTION TOOL

The Data-Collection Tool helps you gather information about the students' experiences during literacy walks. You create it based on best practices in literacy instruction—specifically, the six essential components of a comprehensive program, K–8:

1. **Read-Aloud**

2. **Shared Reading**

3. **Small-Group and Independent Reading**

4. **Writing**

5. **Word Work**

6. **Language**

In the appendix, pages 100–140, and at scholastic.com/LiteracyWalksResources, you'll find grade-specific "look-fors"—essential and observable elements of instruction—for each of those six components, organized into categories such as:

- Environment
- Print Concepts
- Phonological Awareness
- Phonics
- Conventions
- Engagement
- Fluency
- Comprehension
- Vocabulary
- Composition
- Mechanics
- Listening and Speaking

Here are some examples:

First-grade look-fors for word work/phonological awareness and phonics include:

- Decode (segment and blend) two-syllable words by breaking them into syllables.
- Recognize sound-spelling connections with common consonant digraphs and blends.
- Count and pronounce phonemes in spoken words.
- Isolate and pronounce initial, medial, and final phonemes in single-syllable words.
- Blend phonemes, including consonant blends, into spoken words.
- Make sound-spelling connections with common consonant digraphs (e.g., *th*) and blends (e.g., *st*).
- Blend onsets and rimes.
- Decode long-vowel sounds in regularly spelled one-syllable words (final -*e* and common vowel teams).
- Know that every syllable in a word must have a vowel sound.
- Read words with inflectional endings (e.g., -*s*, -*er*, -*ing*).

Fourth-grade look-fors for small-group and independent reading/comprehension include:

- Make predictions about what will happen next in the story based on details and prior knowledge of the text.
- Refer to details and examples in a text when explaining what it says explicitly.
- Draw inferences from a text, using details from the text to support them.
- Summarize the text using details and information drawn from it.
- Describe in depth a character (traits, thoughts, actions), setting, or event in a story or drama, drawing on specific details.
- Compare and contrast the point of view from which different stories are narrated, including first and third person.
- Compare and contrast themes and topics (e.g., good vs. evil) across more than two texts.
- Explain how an author uses reasons and evidence to support points.
- Integrate information from two texts on the same topic to write or speak about the topic knowledgeably.
- Explain events, procedures, ideas, or concepts in a historical, scientific, or technical text, including what happened and why, based on text details.

Sixth-grade look-fors for writing/composition include:

- Link ideas and information using words and phrases.
- Develop topics with examples, facts, definitions, quotes, and information that references what they have read or researched.
- With narrative writing, use effective techniques, relevant descriptive details, and well-structured sequence of events.
- With explanatory, descriptive, or informative writing, introduce and examine a topic.

- Convey ideas, concepts, and information through the selection and organization of relevant content.
- Carefully choose relevant content to include in the writing.
- With explanatory, descriptive, or informative writing, introduce a topic or thesis statement and group relevant information in paragraphs and sections to support the statement.
- With argument writing, state a claim and provide clear reasons and evidence (i.e., facts and details) for it; organize writing by grouping related ideas to support the claim and including a concluding section or statement.

Eighth-grade look-fors for language/listening and speaking include:

- Students' language or dialect is respected and it is understood that it reflects the identities, values, and experiences of the child's family and community.
- Participate effectively in a range of collaborative discussions (one-on-one, in groups, and teacher-led) with diverse partners.
- Produce and expand complex sentences to express details orally.
- Acknowledge when new information is presented by others and when others modify their views.
- Ask questions that elicit elaboration of ideas to respond to others' thinking, probing others to reflect on their ideas during discussion.
- Explain how ideas presented in diverse media and formats clarify a topic, text, or issue under study.
- Express self in complete and complex sentences.
- Summarize information from texts read aloud or from presentations and viewing multimedia.
- Summarize key points of a speaker and the attitude of the speaker, evaluating the soundness of reasons and relevance of evidence.
- Present claims and findings emphasizing salient points in a focused and cohesive manner with relevant evidence, valid reasoning, and well-chosen details.
- Include multimedia components and visual displays in presentations to clarify claims and findings and emphasize salient points.
- Use complete sentences when discussing, presenting, or responding; report/present opinions and information.
- Delineate a speaker's argument and specific claims, evaluating the soundness of the reasoning and relevance and sufficiency of the evidence and identifying when irrelevant evidence is introduced.
- Present claims and findings (e.g., argument, narrative, response to literature presentations), emphasizing salient points in a focused, coherent manner with relevant evidence, sound valid reasoning, and well-chosen details.

How to Create Your Customized Data-Collection Tool

Follow these instructions to create a Data-Collection Tool tailored to your team's instructional goal.

Data-Collection Tool

Team Goal:

Grade(s):	Teacher(s):	Date(s):

Component(s) to Observe: ☐ Read-Aloud ☐ Shared Reading ☐ Small-Group and Independent Reading ☐ Word Work ☐ Writing ☐ Language

Classroom Arrangement: ☐ Whole-Class ☐ Small Group ☐ Individual

LOOK-FORS BY CATEGORY	TEACHER SAYS/DOES	STUDENTS SAY/DO
[Paste by category look-fors from the bank for you chosen component(s) here.]		

① Go to scholastic.com/LiteracyWalks Resources and download a copy of the Data-Collection Tool template.

② Fill in your team goal, the grade(s) you plan to visit, the teacher(s), and the date.

Data-Collection Tool

Team Goal:
To engage students in discussions about text in which they share big ideas

Grade(s):	Teacher(s):	Date(s):
3	Monero and Jackson	12/2

Component(s) to Observe: ☐ Read-Aloud ☒ Shared Reading ☐ Small-Group and Independent Reading ☒ Word Work ☐ Writing ☐ Language

Classroom Arrangement: ☒ Whole-Class ☐ Small Group ☐ Individual

LOOK-FORS BY CATEGORY	TEACHER SAYS/DOES	STUDENTS SAY/DO

③ Check off the literacy component(s) that you plan to observe (i.e., Read-Aloud, Shared Reading, Small-Group and Independent Reading, Word Work, Writing, and/or Language).

④ Check off the classroom arrangement for that component (i.e., whole-class, small group, individual).

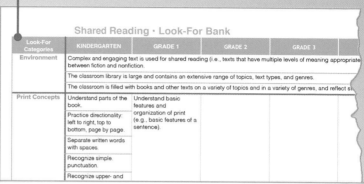

(5) Choose the category or categories for the literacy component(s) you've checked off. For guidance, go to the Look-For Banks at scholastic.com/LiteracyWalksResources.

In this example, the Shared Reading bank includes the look-for categories:

Environment	Fluency
Print Concepts	Comprehension
Phonics	Engagement

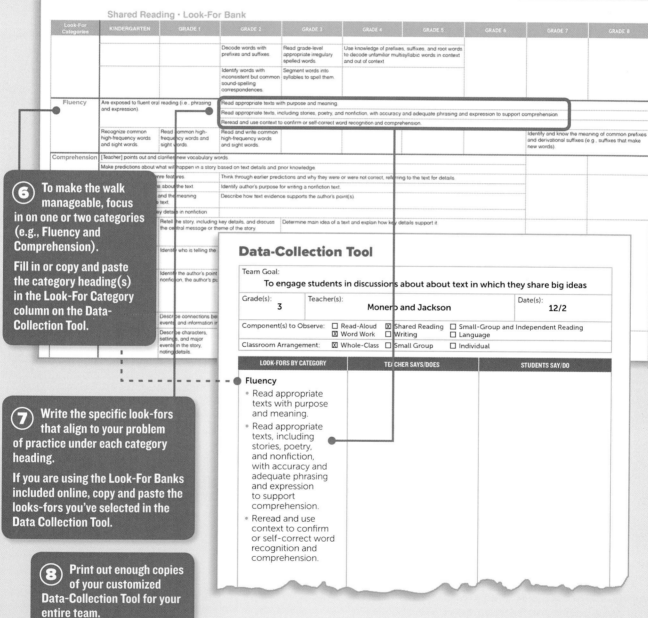

(6) To make the walk manageable, focus in on one or two categories (e.g., Fluency and Comprehension).

Fill in or copy and paste the category heading(s) in the Look-For Category column on the Data-Collection Tool.

(7) Write the specific look-fors that align to your problem of practice under each category heading.

If you are using the Look-For Banks included online, copy and paste the looks-fors you've selected in the Data Collection Tool.

(8) Print out enough copies of your customized Data-Collection Tool for your entire team.

Data-Collection Tool

Team Goal:
To engage students in discussions about about text in which they share big ideas

Grade(s): 3	Teacher(s): Monero and Jackson	Date(s): 12/2

Component(s) to Observe: ☐ Read-Aloud ☒ Shared Reading ☐ Small-Group and Independent Reading ☒ Word Work ☐ Writing ☐ Language

Classroom Arrangement: ☒ Whole-Class ☐ Small Group ☐ Individual

LOOK-FORS BY CATEGORY	TEACHER SAYS/DOES	STUDENTS SAY/DO
Fluency • Read appropriate texts with purpose and meaning. • Read appropriate texts, including stories, poetry, and nonfiction, with accuracy and adequate phrasing and expression to support comprehension. • Reread and use context to confirm or self-correct word recognition and comprehension.		

Data-Collection Tool

Team Goal:		
To engage students in discussions about text in which they share big ideas		

Grade(s):	Teacher(s):	Date(s):
3	**Monero and Jackson**	**12/2**

Component(s) to Observe: ☐ Read-Aloud ☒ Shared Reading ☐ Small-Group and Independent Reading
☒ Word Work ☐ Writing ☐ Language

Classroom Arrangement: ☒ Whole-Class ☐ Small Group ☐ Individual

LOOK-FORS BY CATEGORY	TEACHER SAYS/DOES	STUDENTS SAY/DO
Fluency • Read appropriate texts with purpose and meaning. • Read appropriate texts, including stories, poetry, and nonfiction, with accuracy and adequate phrasing and expression to support comprehension. • Reread and use context to confirm or self-correct word recognition and comprehension. **Comprehension** • Ask questions about the text and explicitly refer to it to answer them. • Describe stories; determine central messages and identify them with details from the text. • Compare and contrast themes, settings, and plots of books in a series. • Describe relationships between ideas, events, concepts, and information in a text, using cause and effect, time and sequence, etc. • Describe logical connections between sentences and paragraphs in a text. • Compare and contrast the most important points and key details in two texts on the same topic. • Use information from words and pictures to describe characters, setting, and plot.		

Completed customized Data-Collection Tool

Data-Collection Tool

Page ____2____

LOOK-FORS BY CATEGORY	TEACHER SAYS/DOES	STUDENTS SAY/DO
Comprehension cont. • Use information from text features (e.g., diagrams, photographs) to understand main points. • Think through earlier predictions and why they were or were not correct, referring to the text for details. • Identify author's purpose for writing a nonfiction text. • Describe how text evidence supports the author's point(s). • Distinguish their own point of view from the narrator's and characters' points of view.		

The customized Data-Collection Tool is designed to be flexible. For example, perhaps your team is working on understanding how shared reading looks across grades two, three, and four. You would schedule walks during shared-reading time across those grades, using a tool you create from the Look-For Bank for shared reading, at scholastic.com/Literacy WalksResources, or that you create by writing in your own look-fors. Afterward, team members would debrief on what they learned about shared reading across the grades.

On the other hand, perhaps your team is working on understanding how multiple components look at a specific time of day, say from 8:30 to 11:00, for grade two. At 8:30, in one teacher's classroom, you might observe shared reading, using a shared-reading tool that you create. At 9:15, in another teacher's classroom, you might observe small-group and independent reading, using a tool created for that component. At 10:00, in yet another teacher's classroom, you might observe word work, using a tool created for word work. By the end of the morning, the team would have a clear picture of the type of teaching and learning going on across second grade. You create the tools based on the team's goal.

> The Data-Collection Tool helps you gather information about the six essential components of a comprehensive literacy program, according to observable elements of instruction (i.e., look-fors). Your team creates a Data-Collection Tool that matches your established instructional goal.

TWO EXAMPLES OF DATA-COLLECTION TOOLS

Take a look at the fifth-grade Data-Collection Tool for small-group and independent reading, below, which is organized into these look-for categories: environment, comprehension, and engagement. The look-fors for those categories work together to ensure the teacher has established a vibrant learning community, is giving students meaning-driven literacy tasks, and is implementing the gradual release model and the teaching-learning-assessing loop.

Data-Collection Tool

Team Goal:	To increase students' ability to read independently		

Grade(s): 5	Teacher(s): Nguyen		Date(s): 4/21

Component(s) to Observe:	☐ Read-Aloud ☐ Word Work	☐ Shared Reading ☐ Writing	☒ Small-Group and Independent Reading ☐ Language
Classroom Arrangement:	☐ Whole-Class	☒ Small Group	☐ Individual

LOOK-FORS BY CATEGORY	TEACHER SAYS/DOES	STUDENTS SAY/DO
Environment • Appropriate text is used including leveled text, decodable text, and language-controlled text. There is a balance between fiction and nonfiction. • Each student has a personalized, individual book bag or box for independent reading. • The classroom library is large and contains an extensive range of topics, text types, and genres. • The classroom is filled with books and other texts on a variety of topics and in a variety of genres, and reflect students' races, cultures, and identities, and those of others. **Comprehension** • [Teacher] points out and clarifies new vocabulary words. • Refer to details and examples in a text when explaining what it says explicitly. • Draw inferences from a text, using details from the text to support them. • Summarize the text using details and information drawn from it. • Describe in depth a character (traits, thoughts, actions), setting, or event in a story or drama, drawing on specific details. • Compare and contrast the point of view from which different stories are narrated, including first and third person.		

Data-Collection Tool

LOOK-FORS BY CATEGORY	TEACHER SAYS/DOES	STUDENTS SAY/DO
Comprehension (cont.) • Compare and contrast themes and topics (e.g., good vs. evil) across more than two texts. • Use Greek and Latin roots and affixes to determine word meanings. • Make predictions about what will happen next in the story based on details and prior knowledge of the text. • Think through earlier predictions and why they did or did not come true, referring to the text explicitly for details. • Identify the author's purpose for writing the text. • Determine themes in a story, drama, or poem from details it contains. • Determine the main idea of a text and explain how key details support it. • Distinguish their own point of view apart from the narrator's and characters' points of view. **Engagement** • Engage in collaborative conversations about text, story, and nonfiction topics. • Are central to the discussion, and do the majority of thinking and talking about texts. • Speak audibly and independently. • Express self in complete sentences. • [Teacher] discusses confusing points or misunderstandings about the text. • [Teacher] discusses new or confusing vocabulary and encourages inferences.		

As you can see in the example below, the second-grade Data-Collection Tool is similar to the fifth-grade tool, but the chosen component is word work, and it's organized into three look-for categories: environment, phonics, and fluency. In contrast to the fifth-grade Data-Collection Tool, word work is broken down by foundational skills (phonemic awareness, phonics, and fluency), making it developmentally appropriate for second grade.

Data-Collection Tool

Team Goal:
To enable students to decode unknown words in order to read independently

Grade(s): **2**	Teacher(s): **Nasir, Williams, and Kwon**	Date(s): **10/2–10/4**

Component(s) to Observe: ☐ Read-Aloud ☐ Shared Reading ☐ Small-Group and Independent Reading
☒ Word Work ☐ Writing ☐ Language

Classroom Arrangement: ☐ Whole-Class ☐ Small Group ☒ Individual

LOOK-FORS BY CATEGORY	TEACHER SAYS/DOES	STUDENTS SAY/DO
Environment • An up-to-date sound wall is present, which students can refer to when reading and writing. **Phonics** • Distinguish long and short vowels in regular one-syllable words (CVCe words). • Know sound-spelling correspondences for common vowel teams. • Decode (segment and blend) two-syllable words with long vowels. • Decode words with prefixes and suffixes. • Identify words with inconsistent but common sound-spelling correspondences. • Distinguish between similarly spelled words by identifying different sounds of letters. • Segment sounds to write words. • Read level-appropriate irregular, but common, words. • Self-monitor and apply word-reading skills to self-correct.		

Data-Collection Tool

LOOK-FORS BY CATEGORY	TEACHER SAYS/DOES	STUDENTS SAY/DO
Fluency • Read and write common high-frequency words and sight words. • Read appropriate texts with purpose and meaning. • Read appropriate texts with accuracy and adequate fluency to support comprehension. • Reread and use context to confirm or self-correct word recognition and understanding.		

Using the Data-Collection Tool on Literacy Walks

As explained in Chapter 4, there are several ways to collect data during a literacy walk—literal notes, descriptive notes, and checklists. Taking descriptive notes provides the opportunity to collect qualitative data about the teaching and learning that's occurring in the classroom. Using predetermined look-fors in the Data-Collection Tools helps you focus on specific practices in a comprehensive literacy program. All the look-fors, organized by literacy component, are available in the appendix, pages 100–140, and at scholastic.com/LiteracyWalksResources.

Let's take a look at a filled-in Data-Collection Tool for kindergarten to get an idea of how to use it.

1 Create a tool that matches the component you're focusing on (e.g., read-aloud, language), following the instructions on pages 44–45. Note that the language look-fors include elements to observe during English Language Development (ELD) lessons.

2 Note the type of lesson you are observing, either whole-class, small group, or individual.

3 Depending on the look-for categories you've chosen, note the level and type of literacy-rich experiences you observe, keeping in mind the classroom environment should support those experiences in a variety of ways—written, oral, and visual. The environment should be vibrant, filled with the sounds of students talking, interacting, and collaborating while learning. Silent classrooms do not encourage deep thinking and processing or develop oral language.

4 Write descriptive notes about what the teacher is saying and doing and what the students are saying and doing, as they relate to the look-fors in the first column.

Data-Collection Tool

Team Goal:	To ensure read-alouds are engaging and develop students' love of reading and ability to share big ideas about text		

Grade(s): K	Teacher(s): Cohen		Date(s): 3/5

1 Component(s) to Observe: ☒ Read-Aloud   ☐ Shared Reading   ☐ Small-Group and Independent Reading
☐ Word Work   ☐ Writing   ☐ Language

2 Classroom Arrangement: ☒ Whole-Class   ☐ Small Group   ☐ Individual

LOOK-FORS BY CATEGORY	TEACHER SAYS/DOES	STUDENTS SAY/DO
3 Print Concepts • Understand parts of the book. • Understand the roles of the author and illustrator. **Fluency** • Are exposed to fluent oral reading (i.e., phrasing and expression). **Comprehension (fiction)** • Recognize and discuss beginnings, middle details, and endings in fiction texts. • Discuss characters and character experiences, thoughts, and feelings. • Discuss new words in group discussion. • Recognize genre and genre features. • Ask and answer questions about the text. • Describe the illustrations and the meaning illustrations provide to the text. **Engagement** • Are central to the discussion, and do the majority of thinking and talking about texts. • Speak audibly and independently. • [Teacher] discusses confusing points or misunderstandings about the text. • [Teacher] discusses words regularly and posts them around the room. • [Teacher] discusses new or confusing vocabulary and encourages inferences. • [Teacher] stops at points in the book to check students' listening comprehension, focusing on *who, what, why, when,* and *where* questions. • [Teacher] stops at points in the book to ask inquiry questions or deep comprehension questions. • [Teacher] encourages talk and responds to what students are saying, rather than correcting how they are saying it.	Mr. Cohen began reading a book by sharing the title. He asked students what they knew about giraffes and made a comment that the giraffe on the cover was a cartoon and not a real giraffe. Mr. Cohen read the text with enthusiasm and once in a while stopped at certain punctuation and discussed the purpose of it. Mr. Cohen described the illustrations on each page, emphasizing new thinking and ideas that appeared in the illustrations. He asked students what they saw in the pictures and asked them to describe the pictures. At two points in the book, Mr. Cohen stopped and asked students what they thought the giraffe was going to do since he was in trouble. He validated each child's idea.	**4** The students were ready to read and were excited about the book. Some of the students moved around a lot on the carpet. Three students in the back became very distracted in the beginning. The students listened intently when the teacher raised his voice to make the reading exciting. Three students raised their hands to share their ideas about the giraffe's troubles. The students also sat knee to knee to share their thinking when prompted, which got all but two of the students talking.

The example below shows what a filled-in Data-Collection Tool for shared reading might look like after completing a literacy walk in a sixth-grade classroom. Notice the note-taker spent the majority of time observing how the students were determining the central idea in the text they were reading and citing specific details to defend their thinking. The descriptive notes paint a picture of what the teacher was doing to support students, and what students were saying in response. They provide detail about what instruction looked like and sounded like. The notes help team members be *in the moment* in a way a check mark in a box cannot.

Data-Collection Tool

Team Goal:	To help students determine the main idea in a text, and cite details to back up their thinking		
Grade(s): 6	**Teacher(s):** Patel		**Date(s):** 4/29–4/30

Component(s) to Observe:	☐ Read-Aloud ☒ Shared Reading ☐ Small-Group and Independent Reading ☐ Word Work ☐ Writing ☐ Language
Classroom Arrangement:	☒ Whole-Class ☐ Small Group ☐ Individual

LOOK-FORS BY CATEGORY	TEACHER SAYS/DOES	STUDENTS SAY/DO
Comprehension • Refer to details and examples in a text when explaining what it says explicitly. • Draw inferences from a text, using details from the text to support them. • Summarize the text using details and information drawn from it. • Describe in depth a character (traits, thoughts, actions), setting, or event in a story or drama, drawing on specific details. • Compare and contrast themes and topics (e.g., good vs. evil) across more than two texts. • Explain how an author uses reasons and evidence to support points. • Compare and contrast a firsthand and secondhand account of an event; describe the differences in focus and the information provided; examine primary documents.	Ms. Patel began by introducing the text. She asked students about one point in the text (about lying) in order to build background knowledge. Ms. Patel stopped after reading with students the first paragraph. She asked, "What do you think the character feels?" She continued reading and stopped periodically to ask the students what they noticed about the characters and how the two main characters relate to one another. She would ask, "What do you think?" At one point, Ms. Patel stopped and asked students to jot down a few notes about their thinking. Then she put the students in groups of three and asked them to come up with one idea about their thinking so far.	Three students shared their experiences with people who lie and expressed their feelings and ideas. Students talked with a partner when prompted by the teacher. They talked together about the characters and what was happening in the relationship between the two main characters. After the pair share, three groups of students discussed what they had talked about. One of the groups read two lines of text that supported their idea. Two students shared their thoughts about the characters' feelings. The students were able to point to sentences in the book that backed up their thinking. There were nine groups of three. Of the nine groups, students in five of them were able to state what they thought the author was trying to tell the readers about how the characters were not honest. Two groups struggled a bit and could not decide on the main idea.

Data-Collection Tool

LOOK-FORS BY CATEGORY	TEACHER SAYS/DOES	STUDENTS SAY/DO
Comprehension (cont.) • Make predictions about what will happen next in the story based on details and prior knowledge of the text. • Think through earlier predictions and why they did or did not come true, referring to the text explicitly for details. • Identify the author's point of view. • Identify the author's purpose for writing the text. • Describe how text evidence supports the author's point(s). • Determine the main idea of a text and explain how key details support it. • Distinguish their own point of view apart from the narrator's and characters' points of view.	After the group work, Ms. Patel asked the group of three to write a summary statement about the central idea in the text so far. It was clear from the anchor chart on the wall in the classroom that she had previously taught about central ideas in a text. Ms. Patel met with the two groups of students that were struggling previously. The students in these two groups were quiet and did not say too much. She gave them a pointer and then said she would check back with them.	Five of the groups were able to come to consensus on the main idea in the text so far. One group argued for a few minutes, but most of the groups worked together. Three of the groups worked on identifying lines in the text that backed up their ideas. Students in those groups highlighted the lines of text that they wanted to share as evidence. All of the groups shared their thinking with the class. One student from each group was the spokesperson for the group. All students did not have a chance to talk this way, which was limiting. At the end of the session, students wrote their ideas in a reading notebook.

Bringing It All Together

In the appendix and at scholastic.com/LiteracyWalksResources, you will find the raw material you need (i.e., look-fors organized by literacy component) to create Data-Collection Tools for grade levels K–8. Use the tools to help your team develop understanding of the literacy instruction that's happening in your school and how students are responding to it. Use them to guide your professional learning.

CHAPTER 6

Taking Time for Professional Learning
Debrief the Literacy Walks

"I thought the best part of the literacy walk was going to be getting to visit my colleague's classroom; I was wrong. The best part is the debrief after the walk. It was exciting to share our data and think about what students were learning. I felt empowered to be on the team that suggested to our principal what our next PD session needed to be."

—DAUS, FIRST-GRADE TEACHER

This chapter discusses how to use the data collected during the literacy walk for focused discussion and reflection. In it, I cover the final two steps in the process:

1. Create the Team
2. Identify a Problem of Practice
3. Establish Your First Instructional Goal
4. Develop Clarity of What Practice Needs to Look Like
5. Organize and Schedule Your Walks
6. Collect Data During the Literacy Walk
7. **Debrief With the Team About Observations**
8. **Choose a New Instructional Goal**

Step 7: Debrief With the Team About Observations

After each literacy walk, debrief with your team for about an hour. By discussing what you noticed and noted, you will be preparing yourselves for an open conversation based on the data you collected. (See Chapters 4 and 5 for guidelines on note taking and data collection.) Be sure to stay focused on what the notes indicate—and, from there, make plans to tweak existing instructional strategies and techniques, and try out new ones (Curtis & City, 2009).

PLAN A MEETING

Preferably, the debrief meeting happens on the same day as the walk, ideally at lunch or right after school, so that everyone's memories are fresh and outlooks are bright from working with and learning from each other. It is fine to debrief on another day, if necessary, but choose a day as close as possible to the day of the walk.

ENDEAVOR ELEMENTARY SCHOOL

AGENDA for a PM Team Debrief Meeting

- The AM team debriefed at lunch. The PM team will debrief immediately after school.
- Teams will present findings at the next staff meeting, which the entire faculty will discuss.

2:30	Part I	Organize evidence individually.
2:45	Part II	In small groups, share evidence and discuss patterns and trends.
3:00	Part III	In small groups, debrief and make predictions.
3:15	Part IV	As a whole group, review final statements and decide on the next goal.

USE AN AFFINITY DIAGRAM PROTOCOL

The debrief meeting works best if you use an affinity diagram protocol, which allows for all voices to be heard and for multiple perspectives to surface. It also ensures some anonymity because participants put their thoughts on sticky notes and post them on a large piece of chart paper. Once all the notes are posted, participants group and regroup them, unaware of who wrote what. The goal is to identify themes among the notes (Bernhardt, 2017). There are seven steps. Participants:

1. Settle into a group and review the established goal of the walk and then review the data.

2. Identify particularly interesting or useful observations and jot them down on sticky notes.

3. Get into small groups and share sticky notes by reading them aloud and posting them on a large piece of chart paper.

Data-Collection Tool

Team Goal:	To help students determine the main idea in a text, and cite details to back up their thinking		

Grade(s): 6	Teacher(s): Patel		Date(s): 4/29–4/30

Component(s) to Observe:	☐ Read-Aloud ☒ Shared Reading ☐ Small-Group and Independent Reading
	☐ Word Work ☐ Writing ☐ Language
Classroom Arrangement:	☒ Whole-Class ☐ Small Group ☐ Individual

LOOK-FORS BY CATEGORY	TEACHER SAYS/DOES	STUDENTS SAY/DO
Comprehension • Refer to details and examples in a text when explaining what it says explicitly. • Draw inferences from a text, using details from the text to support them. • Summarize the text using details and information drawn from it. • Describe in depth a character (traits, thoughts, actions), setting, or event in a story or drama, drawing on specific details. • Compare and contrast themes and topics (e.g., good vs. evil) across more than two texts.	Ms. Patel began by introducing the text. She asked stude[nts]... point in the text... in order to build [background] knowledge. Ms. Patel stoppe[d] reading with stu[dents]... paragraph. She asked, "What do you think the character feels?" She continued reading and stopped periodically to ask the students what t[hey]... about the chara[cters]... the two main cha[racters]... to one another. S[he asked]... "What do you thi[nk]..." *Students took turns adding on to each other's thinking about the book when the teacher paused for comments.* *19 out of 20 students participated in discussion about the book. During discussion they talked about the meaning of the book.*	Three students shared their experience with people who lie and expressed their feelings and ideas. Students talked with a partner when prompted by the teacher. They talked toget[her]... the characters a[nd]... happening in the [story]... between the two... characters. After the pair sha[red]... groups of students discussed what they had talked about. One of the groups read two lines of text that backup up their idea. *The teacher provided wait time for the students to think before she asked them to share their thoughts about the text.*

4. Group the sticky notes by common themes. Label each group of notes with its theme.

5. Look for trends that emerge from grouping the sticky notes, and make a clear statement or two about them.

6. Reconvene with the team. A representative from each small group shares its statement(s) and expands on it, based on observations during the walk.

STEPS IN A TYPICAL DEBRIEF MEETING

WHOLE GROUP
Review goal and collected data, identify observations and jot them on sticky notes.

→

SMALL GROUP
Share sticky notes, group for themes, notice trends, make statements about trends.

→

WHOLE GROUP
Note overall trends and decide on a new goal.

7. Decide on a new goal for their ongoing effort to improve literacy instruction.

Each Step in Detail

1. Whole Group

Review the established goal and then review notes and data. Gather everyone together and provide materials to make your meeting a success, including chart paper, markers, highlighters, and lots of sticky notes. Review the established goal and then ask participants to look at their notes and highlight, underline, or star points that are especially salient, notable, or interesting in relation to the goal.

Jot down particularly interesting or useful observations on sticky notes. Invite participants to look at observations they highlighted and write them on the sticky notes, one observation per sticky note. It is fine to summarize observations—for instance, "In 10 of 12 classrooms, students were reading independently"—but those that are captured verbatim are often more powerful. Participants should jot down about eight to ten observations because the more data the group has to consider, the more accurate the team's understanding of the school's current reality will be.

2. Small Group

Share sticky notes in small groups. The meeting's facilitator organizes participants into small groups. Each group is given a sheet of chart paper. Members gather around the chart paper and share their sticky notes with each other, taking turns reading them out loud and placing them on the chart. Turn-taking ensures all voices are heard

Staff development takes time, and instructional practice is never perfect. What's important is noticing what you are doing, what you are not doing, and how students' learning is affected.

and that group members are attentive. Resist grouping the sticky notes; just scatter them on the paper. The goal is to have all voices in the room heard, with each person sharing 10–12 points that they noted and copied from their notes.

Group notes by theme and label them. The small group takes a step back and looks at the sticky notes. Members then collaborate to group the notes thematically and label the grouped notes. The more detailed the labels, the clearer they'll be. For instance, the label *"Students read self-selected book independently during small-group instruction"* is clearer than *"Students working independently."*

Look for trends and make a clear statement or two about them. Based on trends that emerge from grouped notes, members make one or two clear statements about what literacy practices are implemented, to what degree they are implemented, and how implementation is furthering student learning. Members also make a statement about how students were engaged in reading and writing, and discuss their thinking.

Sample Statements:

"In most classrooms, 75 percent of students could capture their reading comprehension in a notebook by recording what the text explicitly said."

"In 7 out of 10 classrooms, during shared reading, nearly all students were able to talk about the text collaboratively in large or small groups."

3. Whole Group

Reconvene as a team and share statements. After the small groups are finished writing their statements, they come back together in a large group. An appointed member from each group shares her group's statements, discusses their thinking, and provides examples from the sticky notes if necessary for clarity. After all the groups share, the participants reflect on similarities and differences between the statements. More similarities will likely emerge than differences, which will inform new directions in practice for the team to move toward. Keeping student success in mind (i.e., what has been working for students and not working for them), participants collaborate on a clear statement or two about what literacy practices are being implemented, to what degree things are implemented, and how implementation is furthering student learning. Doing that creates clarity about the current reality of literacy teaching and learning so that everyone can see, based on the data collected during the literacy walks, what is actually happening in classrooms. The final statement(s) may not be glowing, or as positive as the team had hoped, but that's okay. Staff development takes time, and instructional practice is never perfect. What's important is noticing what you are doing, what you are not doing, and how students' learning is affected.

Directions for a Literacy Walk

LITERACY WALK/OBSERVATIONS

Each team visits four classrooms for about 20 minutes, focusing mainly on these questions:

- What are the students being asked to do?
- What are the teachers saying and doing?
- What are the students saying and doing?

PART I: ON YOUR OWN (ABOUT 15 MINUTES)

- Read through your notes.
- Highlight pieces of evidence that seem relevant to the school focus, or team goal.
- Select 8–10 pieces of evidence. Write down only ONE piece of evidence per sticky note.

PART II: WITH YOUR SMALL GROUP (ABOUT 30 MINUTES)

- Share evidence of each classroom you visited (taking turns). Everyone speaks once before someone speaks twice. Help each other stay in the descriptive voice. What did you see/hear? What makes you think that?
- On chart paper, group the evidence in ways that make sense to each person in the group. Single pieces of evidence can also be a "group." If a piece of evidence belongs in more than one group, copy it onto multiple sticky notes. In essence, the small groups are making categories, but the whole team needs to make the decisions together.
- Label your groupings.
- Identify patterns/trends.
- Identify other relevant or important evidence.
- Write one or two statements on the chart paper about what was noticed during the walk, in relation to the problem of practice, and how implementation is furthering student learning. The group also writes a statement about the extent to which students were engaged in reading, writing, speaking, listening, thinking, and discussing their thinking.

PART III: DEBRIEF AS A WHOLE GROUP (ABOUT 30-40 MINUTES)

- Merge teams into one large group. Have a representative from each team share statements.
- Ask the whole group to work together to write a summary statement. Write a summary statement on the chart paper about what literacy practices are implemented, to what degree things are implemented, and how implementation is furthering student learning (this should relate to the school's problem of practice). Then, organize the statements into one summary statement.
- Ask the group to also make a statement about how students were engaged in reading, writing, and discussing their thinking.
- Set a new goal for the group based on the statement(s).
- Ask, *What is the next step to implement relating to the new goal? What professional development is needed for group learning regarding the new goal?* Record suggestions on chart paper.

(Adapted from Bernhardt, 2017; City, Elmore, Fiarman & Teitel, 2009)

Step 8: Choose a New Instructional Goal

The seven steps of the literacy walk process discussed thus far guide the team through the continuous learning cycle described and illustrated on page 17, from observing practices and examining data to the final step: setting a new goal, based on what was discussed during the debrief meeting. (Hall & Hord, 2019). The goal may vary depending on grade level and content area, and that is fine as long as it focuses on a problem of practice. For example, a goal may be, "To help students engage in collaborative discussions during shared reading and generate significant ideas related to the text." It might emerge right away, or it might take a few days for team members to come up with it. Take the time you need to arrive at a goal that will benefit students, teachers, and the school community most. See Chapter 2 for more information on establishing a goal.

Once the goal is set, the team needs to decide what it is going to focus on first. You don't want to set too many steps for implementation of the goal as it will then be hard to achieve the goal. It is better to set small steps that you can achieve, and then move onto another practice in the future. Developing ideas about how to learn what needs to shift with instruction is important. The team members won't leave the literacy walk debrief suddenly knowing how to implement the next step; there needs to be time for group learning.

Actions the team can choose to help them with learning next steps to reach the goal include:

- Engaging in a book study of a professional text.
- Organizing professional development sessions.
- Having experts on the team lead professional development.
- Bringing in outside experts to lead professional development.
- Implementing lesson study.
- Watching each other teach.
- Videotaping of lessons to watch individually or in teams.
- Examining student work in teams after a specific lesson, or sequence of lessons.

Bringing It All Together

During the debrief, the team comes together to learn from the data collected during the literacy walk. In this chapter, I discussed how to organize the data for the debrief meeting and make sense of it. My process of building trust creates room for all team members to feel their voices and their ideas are being heard in sharing data. That said, be sure to tweak the process as necessary to best fit the needs of your team.

PART III
AFTER THE WALK

Coaching to Improve Teacher and Student Learning

CHAPTER 7

Supporting Instruction
Side-by-Side Coaching
After Literacy Walks

"I think the biggest thing is having somebody with expertise who knows the students, to sit side-by-side [with teachers] and take a look at what instruction looks like and help them be reflective."

—MERCEDES, FIFTH-GRADE TEACHER

Literacy walks are about supporting individual teachers' growth, and the growth of the school culture and community. The process, as I've discussed thus far, includes setting a goal, collecting data, reflecting on data, and setting a new goal. But goal setting is not enough. Teachers need professional development to become expert in new techniques and practices, and instructional coaching is a great way to do that. If you are a school administrator or instructional coach, you are in the perfect position to support the work that comes after the literacy walk.

Research shows a strong correlation between instructional coaching and student achievement. There's also a strong correlation between teacher efficacy (the extent to which we believe we can accomplish what we intend in our teaching) and academic emphasis (the extent to which we emphasize high-level learning for students). Furthermore, the best coaching is side-by-side coaching (Akhavan, 2011), meaning coaching provided by a peer, instructional coach, or leader who is by the teacher's side as she or he expresses thoughts, asks questions, and reflects. In side-by-side coaching, the coach is an equal, not an evaluator, nor "expert." Teachers can be vulnerable and take risks during side-by-side coaching because the coach is there to encourage and bolster them.

Literacy walks are only as successful as what the team does together *after* them. If you are going to lean on someone to help you grow in your practice, who better to lean on than your peers and colleagues (Mierink, Imants, Meijer & Verloop, 2010; Tillema, 2007)?

Coaching After Literacy Walks

As the coach, it is sometimes difficult to know what actions to take. But it's easier if you remain focused on facilitating learning so that each teacher can grow, along with the school culture and community. Of course, you cannot simply tell teachers what to do. You need to be open to learning, too, alongside the teachers (Knight, 2017). Everyone involved in literacy walks should grow together as a team, and for that to happen, your coaching needs to focus on learning, not compliance.

Sara was a high school teacher I worked with who had been asked by her principal to change her instruction based on the problem of practice the team was working on. She was reading texts to students and not engaging them in a close reading. I watched her teach a lesson one day, and noticed her frustration and borderline anger coming through. Later in the day we grabbed a cup of coffee together and I asked her about how she was feeling. She was surprised. She thought I was going to tell her what she did right or wrong in the lesson. I told her that I truly wanted to know how she was feeling, and that I was not there to tell her what she was doing correctly or incorrectly. She then burst into tears. After she composed herself, she admitted to feeling so much pressure after receiving her principal's directive that she was going through the motions of implementing close reading, as her team had decided, but she felt she didn't know what she was doing. Sara was complying. She was not learning; she was simply reacting. In the end, I was able to help the principal understand and more appropriately respond to Sara's challenges through a Concerns-Based Adoption model I introduce later in the chapter.

In this chapter, I discuss coaching models to consider after literacy walks: side-by-side coaching, directive coaching, reflective coaching, inquiry coaching, invitational coaching, and the concerns-based adoption model. According to Taylor and Chanter (2019), the coach should be flexible and responsive to the needs of the teacher and the context in which the coaching is occurring. Coaching might be directive or guiding as necessary or collaborative and open-ended.

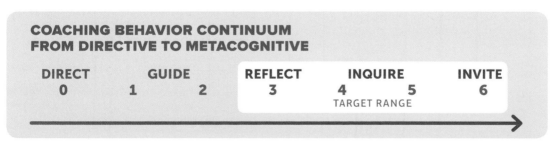

COACHING BEHAVIOR CONTINUUM FROM DIRECTIVE TO METACOGNITIVE

DIRECT		GUIDE		REFLECT	INQUIRE		INVITE
0	1	2		3	4	5	6

TARGET RANGE

Taylor & Chanter, 2019

Side-by-Side Coaching

Side-by-side coaching is reflective, inquiry-based, and also invitational. When coaches and teachers sit side by side, they have:

- opportunities to learn something new together.
- time to openly reflect on what is occurring during instruction.
- strong cooperation and teamwork.
- equal status (Akhavan, 2011).

The coach does everything she can to be honest and "real" with the teacher. She enters the relationship as a learner and colleague, as a fellow educator rather than an authority figure. Sitting side by side is an act of respect, care, and equality. Teachers are more willing to try new instructional practices with a supportive person beside them—someone who encourages and accepts them as they are—rather than a seemingly perfect, potentially judgmental person.

COMPASSIONATE COMMUNICATION DURING SIDE-BY-SIDE COACHING

There is more to coaching than telling a teacher what to do in his classroom. When you engage in side-by-side coaching, it's important to engage in "compassionate communication," an approach that leads us to be open to the teacher and more giving of ourselves (Rosenberg, 2015). Compassionate communication leads to greater outcomes because the teacher is an active participant in the problem-solving process. When we are open and giving, we are able to connect to whomever we're speaking in positive ways (Akhavan, 2011).

Compassionate communication involves observing without evaluating. When coaching side by side, we can certainly make observations and reflect on what we saw and heard, but we shouldn't make value statements. For instance, if a team decides during the debrief meeting to focus on language development during guided instruction, the coach could visit the teachers' classrooms to observe a lesson. After a lesson in which the children read a book on bears, she might say, "I noticed that you spent several minutes engaging students in a discussion about types of bears prior to reading, which generated a lot of words and concepts related to bears. Then, while reading the book together, you asked questions that required students to think back to those words and concepts, which tells me that your pre-reading instruction helped students comprehend the text."

Notice how the coach made a statement about what she observed and how it contributed to students' positive reading experience. The coach did not evaluate by saying, "I noticed that you spent several minutes teaching about different types of bears. I think that was really good and I liked that a lot. " Notice how the second statement is evaluative and doesn't shed light on what the teacher did that was valuable in a non-judgmental way (Aguilar, 2013).

Everyone involved in literacy walks should grow together as a team, and for that to happen, your coaching needs to focus on learning, not compliance.

> **PRACTICE COMPASSIONATE COMMUNICATION BY:**
> - Stating what you observe or notice.
> - Stating what you hear teachers and students saying.
> - Indicating the outcome of what teachers or students said or did by stating another observable fact.
> - Avoiding evaluation or judgment of the teacher's actions and words.
> - Recognizing something the teacher did that led to positive outcomes, based on the identified problem of practice and/or determined goal.
> - Reflecting on an outcome that confirms you reached the goal—or didn't reach it.

Compassionate communication requires us to be present, to listen to others fully, and to validate others as evidence that we are truly listening (Aguilar, 2013; Rosenberg, 2015). When we pay close attention to what a person is saying, with compassion, we don't worry about what we say in response. Asking clarifying questions is part of compassionate communication—questions that help the person reveal more of what he or she is thinking, feeling, or experiencing, and do not belittle or judge. Here's an example of an exchange about shared reading, between a teacher and coach. Notice how the coach listens, asks clarifying questions, and validates what the teacher says.

Teacher	I tried shared reading three times last week, but the week before I only got to it twice.
Coach	Tell me more about that. How did it go?
Teacher	Well, the first week I felt very awkward. I don't think I am very good at shared reading yet.
Coach	What makes you feel that you are not very good at it?
Teacher	Well, my class became very fidgety after about 10 minutes. I started rushing to the end of the text just to get through it.
Coach	When the students became fidgety, you must have felt unsure, and then you felt you had to rush to finish.
Teacher	Yes. The students weren't doing the talking, I kept having to answer my own questions, and they were not engaged.
Coach	Tell me more about how you stopped during the reading and asked questions.

The coach is open to hearing about the teacher's experience, listens carefully, and does not judge. She asks clarifying questions, inviting the teacher to share details, and validates the teacher for her experiences and feelings. This trusting exchange positions the coach and teacher to work on a top concern that will address the problem of practice.

Moving Beyond Side-by-Side Coaching

As mentioned earlier, the team establishes a goal at the end of the debrief meeting, which provides a focus for coaching. However, the coaching should not just focus on implementing what the team said; the coach needs to ask the teacher about her needs. The coach can adapt her approach based on the teacher's needs. She should strive to understand the teacher's perspective before deciding on the approach to take.

DIRECTIVE COACHING

During directive coaching, a coach gives explicit directions, recommendations, or advice by setting the goals for the coaching experience (Aguilar, 2013). This type of coaching doesn't focus on the teacher choosing the goal, because the teacher may not be ready or able to direct his own learning. If you do give advice during directive coaching, make sure it is caring, open, honest, and well-timed (Rosenberg, 2015). For example, a coach might say, "You need to organize reading groups and have that done by next week. It will help to differentiate instruction. How can I help you do this?" If you hear a lot of "yes-buts" from the teacher, or he debates everything you say, stop giving advice (Hargrove, 2008).

GUIDING COACHING

Guiding coaching is helpful for teachers who are new to the profession or new to certain instructional practices or techniques. During guiding coaching, the coach listens carefully to the teacher and may provide pointers on best practices. She may give the teacher curriculum materials, lesson plans, and templates (Aguilar, 2013). She may point out actions the teacher can take. For example, the coach might say, "I noticed you asked thoughtful questions to get students talking about the reading, but the students didn't start talking right away. Do you think it would help to write the question on the whiteboard so students can refer to it?"

The coach may ask the teacher to think about how she would like to see her students' behaviors and learning during a particular lesson. This kind of anticipatory thinking helps to develop the teacher's capacity to consider her practice and prepares her for reflective coaching, the next coaching behavior on the coaching continuum.

> **DURING GUIDING COACHING, YOU MIGHT:**
> - Provide curriculum materials, lesson plans, and templates.
> - Point out what to do or how to do something.
> - Provide information about what comes next instructionally.
> - Ask the teacher questions about her instructional planning. Her answers will help you determine her needs.

REFLECTIVE COACHING

With reflective coaching, the coach supports the teacher through reflection and conversation. In essence, she helps the teacher rewire his beliefs about his instruction and its impact. For that reason, reflective coaching requires patience and compassion. Because teachers involved in a coaching relationship are at different points in their development and bring a wide range of experiences to their learning, the coach can draw out the teacher's needs through reflective questions (Johnston, Dozier & Smit, 2016).

First, the coach guides the teacher to set a goal. If coaching after literacy walks, that goal would relate to the team goal established during the debrief meeting. The coach guides the teacher to achieve the goal by breaking it down into actionable steps that she negotiates with the teacher. As the teacher carries out the steps, the coach discusses the outcomes with him and encourages him to reflect. The coach might then encourage the teacher to identify any barriers or problems with implementing instruction, and think through ways to overcome those issues. She also reviews overall progress with the teacher by asking him to reflect on his actions and how they affected student learning.

Don't hold back on exploring issues. The more you talk about them, the more likely you are to uncover truths and interests (Langer & Moldoveanu, 2000). Encouraging the teacher to drill down deeply on what is actually happening during instruction increases his engagement and positions him as an active, intentional person who generates knowledge about his instruction (Johnston, Dozier & Smit, 2016). The teacher doesn't need to be told (as in directive coaching). Instead, he discovers for himself. This improves the coaching relationship because, as the teacher makes observations about his practice, you, the coach, develop an appreciation of his learning, and your relationship becomes more positive and trusting.

> **Encouraging the teacher to drill down deeply on what is actually happening during instruction increases his engagement and positions him as an active, intentional person who generates knowledge about his instruction.**

DURING REFLECTIVE COACHING, YOU MIGHT ASK:

- Can you tell me what you want to accomplish?
- How do you think you might go about that?
- Based on what has worked or not worked for you in the past, what steps could you take to implement what you are thinking about?
- How did it go? (after trying something new)
- What do you think went well? What didn't go so well?
- What would you do again or change?
- Think about the changes you have made. Which ones have had the greatest impact? Which do you want to keep doing? Which would you abandon? (after trying a series of lessons using a new technique or strategy)

INQUIRY COACHING

Like reflective coaching, inquiry coaching can lead to a transformation in beliefs and attitudes, as well as instructional practice. The coach inquires about a teacher's thoughts, feelings, and experiences, and encourages the teacher to investigate what works or doesn't work for her. For example, an experienced teacher may be interested in trying a new technique inspired by a literacy walk. Because she is experienced, she is normally quite reflective in her practice and often thinks through how her instruction is impacting her students. Therefore, she doesn't need reflective coaching. What she needs is guidance in beginning an inquiry into her own practices and discovering what she knows, as a developing expert, and how she can best apply the new technique to meet her students' needs.

Inquiry into classroom practices is a type of action research. When a teacher carries out action research, she makes inquiries into her practices with the goal of discovering changes that need to be made that will positively impact student learning. It leads her to self-discovery. A coach may help the teacher set up her action research plan. While carrying out the plan, the teacher may focus on personal learning in addition to understanding the outcomes of the instructional changes she's making (Knight, 2017).

> When a teacher carries out action research, she makes inquiries into her practices with the goal of discovering changes that need to be made that will positively impact student learning. It leads her to self-discovery.

WAYS TO BOOST PERSONAL LEARNING

- Focus attention on the here and now.
- Pay close attention to your instruction and note what you are doing and what students are doing in reaction to it.
- Be receptive to what you are noticing. Don't judge yourself or your students.
- Don't emphasize what you "should have" done. Instead, learn from what you did.

(Law, 2013)

The first step in inquiry coaching is to guide the teacher to ask a question about her instruction—a question related to something that's affecting student learning and in what ways. If the coaching is happening after literacy walks, the question would relate to the team goal. For example, if the goal of the walks was to improve read-alouds, the teacher might ask, "What guides students to engage in discussion during read-alouds, and internalize understanding of story elements?"

Next, the coach and teacher would discuss evidence that might be available to understand the effects of instruction. For example, the teacher might check for understanding by having students write their thoughts about her read-aloud on a whiteboard so she can see what each of them is thinking about characters. Essentially, the teacher chooses a data-collection method in order to gather evidence to answer her question (Stake, 1995). From there, the coach gets together with the teacher to discuss her thinking about the data, encouraging her to analyze it and summarize its implications for instruction (Boudette, City, & Murnane, 2013). The goal of the final conversation is to answer the teacher's inquiry question.

> **DURING INQUIRY COACHING, BE SURE TO:**
> - Guide the teacher to think of a question she has that relates to the literacy walk team goal.
> - Assist the teacher in setting up an inquiry by deciding on the instructional steps to take and the data to collect.
> - Once the teacher collects the data, have her analyze it to gain insight on student learning.
> - Ask her to reflect on what she learned about herself. In what ways would she maintain or change her practice, based on the data?
> - Help the teacher answer her research question and set the next instructional step for her to take.

INVITATIONAL COACHING

Invitational coaching is the most self-directed form of coaching on the continuum. Invitational coaching is interactional. The coach invites the teacher to participate in a shared learning experience about her practice. Both the coach and the teacher learn from the experience. If the coach is a fellow teacher, she may also end up changing her own teaching practices based on what she and the teacher discover. Invitational coaching involves helping the teacher to figure out and implement actions to take to help students learn (Harvey, 2015). Rather than tell the teacher what to do, the coach leads the teacher to develop her ability to learn. The coach views the teacher as expert (Harvey, 2015).

Because invitational coaching is based on the coach inviting the teacher to participate in self-directed learning, he or she needs to respect the teacher's willingness to meet. So it's important to check in with the teacher from time to time to see if she wants to continue the coaching or modify it in some way.

Creative tension is that desire we feel when we want to learn something new but don't yet have the skills. It builds when we look closely at what is going on in our classrooms in terms of processes, atmosphere, and student learning, and when we envision how it might look differently in the future. People with high levels of personal mastery:

- Are lifelong learners, continually expanding their ability to create the life they truly seek (Senge, 1990).
- Habitually clarify their personal vision.
- See current reality clearly.
- Know how to generate "creative tension" by understanding current reality and setting goals for growth.

With invitational coaching, the goals should be established by the teacher, not the coach. The coach needs to set aside her hopes and wishes and let the teacher refine her own choices and desires. The coach may ask herself, "What part am I playing in the teacher's choice-making?" (Harvey, 2015). If she realizes she is dominating, she needs to step back and focus on the teacher's self-discovery and refinement of ideas. By reflecting and acting on thoughts that he has about instruction, the teacher is, in essence, engaged in action research, which provides a platform for the teacher to learn on his own. It is the coach's responsibility to guide the teacher through the process.

DURING INVITATIONAL COACHING, BE SURE TO:

- Invite the teacher to participate in a coaching experience.
- Keep your hopes and desires in check so you don't overly influence the teacher.
- Prioritize the teacher's choices and desires.
- Set an instructional goal together that the teacher will implement.
- Invite the teacher to reflect on what he has been practicing, and listen to learn and reflect.
- Ask the teacher to reflect on the outcomes of his teaching practices to uncover new ideas and information.
- Consider changing your own practices based on what you have learned from working with the teacher.

The Concerns-Based Adoption Model

Now that we have explored types of coaching, it is time to focus on how a teacher might go through the process of changing his or her instructional practices and how to address the feelings he or she might have during that process. The Concerns-Based Adoption Model by Hall and Hord (2019) sheds light on the teacher's personal experience in implementing new practices or instructional techniques, based on the team goal established in the literacy walk debrief meeting. There are two parts to the model: the stages of concern that the teacher moves through when implementing the practice or technique and the level of use of that practice or technique (i.e., what the teacher is actually doing to meet the goal).

STAGES OF CONCERN

Frances Fuller (1969) first proposed using the term *concerns* to describe one's feelings and perceptions. This is an important point because being asked to do something new, or differently, in the classroom can cause us to have concerns. Compassionate coaching validates our feelings, and good coaches understand that the work that we are doing is not separate from how we feel about that work. When we feel good about it, efficacy in our work grows (Bandura, 1977). Hall and Hord (2019) identified seven stages of concern (see the following chart). When a coach understands those seven stages, she is more likely to respond with empathy.

CONCERNS-BASED ADOPTION MODEL
Stages of Concern

	Stage of Concern	Expression of Concern	Example
7	Refocusing	I have some ideas about something that would work even better.	I am excited! I know that by tweaking the pacing chart, I can bring more vocabulary instruction.
6	Collaboration	How can I relate what I am doing to what others are doing?	Let's get together and do vertical articulation and integration.
5	Consequence	How is my teaching affecting learners? How can I refine it to have more impact?	Wow! As I reflect on my lesson, the student work indicates that they didn't get it. I need to adjust.
4	Management	I seem to be spending all my time getting materials ready.	There are so many points to the text-based questions and content literacy. I'm not sure I can handle it.
3	Personal	How will using it affect me?	I was just feeling comfortable with the blended learning. Now something new...
2	Informational	I would like to know more about it.	You've been piloting text-based questions and content literacy? I am thinking I want to read a book about them.
1	Unconcerned	I am not concerned about it.	Never heard of content area literacy.

Adapted from Hall and Hord, 2019

When adopting a new practice, teachers often experience the stages of concern along a continuum. First, they typically consider how implementation of a new practice will affect them. They then think about how to manage the essentials needed to implement the practice. Eventually they become concerned about how the practice or technique will impact students and their learning. Beyond that, their concern shifts to their colleagues and understanding how they are responding to it. Ultimately, they reach a stage where they bring their own ideas to the practice or technique.

LEVELS OF USE

The second part of the Concerns-Based Adoption Model is about levels of use of the new instructional technique or practice. During the debrief meeting following the literacy walks, the team decides on a new instructional goal. If the team agrees on the goal, then, presumably, all members are on board. However, being on board with a goal is not enough to make change. You have to make a concerted effort to reach the goal.

Levels of use can help us identify where teachers are in the process of implementation. After all, each of us tends to do things in our own way and in our own time. When working with a teacher, it is important for the coach to identify to what extent the teacher is comfortable with implementation, and in so doing offer the right kind of support.

Levels of use range from "non-use" of the practice or technique, because the teacher doesn't have the information about the practice or technique that she needs to implement it, to "renewal," wherein the teacher fully integrates the practice into her teaching (as described in the chart below).

Trying out the new practice or technique can often take a lot of time and effort, like learning to ride a bicycle. But as the teacher grows, she's likely to become comfortable with the practice and technique and will begin to reflect on it and refine the way she implements it. Eventually, she may consult colleagues to learn about the practice or technique, and refine it by working together.

CONCERNS-BASED ADOPTION MODEL
Levels of Use

Level of Use	Behavioral Indicator of Level	Example
7 Renewal	The user is seeking more effective alternatives to the established use of innovation.	I'm integrating text-based questions and content literacy on the Solar System with my expository reading and writing in 7th grade science.
6 Integration	The user is making deliberate efforts to coordinate with others in using the innovation.	I'm organizing my intermediate team to share our pacing articulation vertically, and add vocabulary instruction.
6 Refinement	The user is making changes to increase outcomes.	Since some parts of the text-based questions and content literacy materials have gaps, I'm supplementing with new ideas.
5 Routine Use	The user is making few or no changes and has an established pattern of use.	I've fully implemented text-based questions and content literacy with fidelity.
4 Mechanical Use	The user is making changes to better organize use of the innovation.	I've tabbed and labeled my manuals.
3 Preparation	The user has definite plans to begin using the innovation.	Next week I'm going to lay it all out and put text-based questions and content literacy into my lesson plans.
2 Orientation	The user is taking initiative to learn more about the innovation.	I'm going to PD this summer.
1 Nonuse	The user has no interest, is taking no action.	I'm not planning anything new or different in reading.

Adapted from Hall and Hord, 2019

APPLYING THE CONCERNS-BASED ADOPTION MODEL DURING COACHING

The relationship between a coach and a teacher should be reciprocal. As coach, you need to listen to the concerns and appreciate the commitments that the teacher brings to that relationship. When sitting side by side, ask the teacher sensitive, open-ended questions to understand his needs and desires for being coached. Ask questions about what is going on in his classroom as it relates to the team goal, and the teaching practices and techniques he's implementing to reach the goal. The teacher's answers to your questions will help you understand his level of use in working toward the team goal and how he feels about the work. It is important to suspend judgment, recognizing that the teachers on the team will be in different places. Pay attention to the person you are coaching and how to help him. Be curious about and open to his teaching practices. Don't force the implementation in the way you think is best. The teacher needs to find his own way (Rosenberg, 2015).

During your discussion, reflect with the teacher on modifications he may need to make in his instruction. With your help, he will be able to see his concerns, and clearly express his feelings. Together, set a goal to help him raise his comfort level and increase his level of use.

When I met with Sara a second time, the high-school science teacher I discussed earlier who was struggling to implement close reading, I was relieved to hear that her principal had apologized and changed his way of supporting her. As a result, Sara was more open to developing her expertise in teaching close reading. When we first met, she was at Level 3 of the stages of concern. Her worries were personal, and she questioned whether she could be successful. But as Sara talked about implementing close reading twice a week, I could see she was now at Level 5. She was following the steps of close reading that her team had decided to follow. In fact, she kept a printout of the steps beside her while teaching the lesson. Sara was growing and learning about herself and her ability to teach using close reading, and she was also learning about her students' ability to have deep conversations about text. I was confident that she would continue to grow, learn, and change.

Bringing It All Together

You may be asking yourself, "Where do I begin?" You begin by listening to the teachers. Set up meetings with them to discuss their hopes for themselves, their students, and the work their students do. Discuss how they feel about the team goal and the extent to which they understand it and embrace it. Knowing their needs will help you determine your next steps. Keep in mind that the teachers you are coaching are going to be in different places in the Concerns-Based Adoption Model, based on their feelings and where they are in their implementation of the team goal, and that is okay. You want to help teachers grow and learn from wherever they're starting.

To learn more about coaching, check out *The Coaching Partnership: Collaboration for Systemic Change, Second Edition,* **by Rosemarye T. Taylor and Carol Chanter.**

CHAPTER 8

Co-Coaching
Teachers Coach One Another After Literacy Walks

"One of the best experiences I had this year was working with another teacher on campus. We worked together to plan our lessons after the literacy walks, and our principal even covered our classes twice for us to watch each other teach. Not only did I get better at small-group instruction, I enjoyed working with Damien; we became a team."

—MARISSA, FOURTH-GRADE TEACHER

Literacy walks help you and your colleagues learn about what students are doing in the vibrant language environments you are creating. They are about learning with your team, with a focus on creating a community of practice, where you come together, work to implement effective literacy practices, and then observe students to understand their learning.

When teachers coach teachers, or "co-coach," we increase self-efficacy in implementing comprehensive literacy practices. As we walk and learn together, we identify areas to support each other and help each other grow. If we are going to lean on someone to help us grow in our practice, who better to lean on—and learn from—than other practitioners on the journey (Curtis & City, 2009)?

An Empowering Experience

This type of coaching typically comes *after* the literacy walk debrief meeting. Teachers might get together to discuss next steps in professional development, or work through the Reflection Sheets in Chapter 9. They might focus on the teaching-and-assessing loop, looking at data collected from their classrooms together, and decide where to go next with instruction.

For co-coaching to be truly effective, important foundations need to be in place, the first being trust. Research shows that there's a positive relationship between trust within a school and school improvement (Bryk & Schneider, 2002; Tschannen-Moran, 2004). To develop trust, the teachers working together need to set some norms, which should be written down and revisited regularly.

> **NORMS FOR BUILDING TRUSTING RELATIONSHIPS**
> 1. Keep the discussion between you and the teacher.
> 2. Create a culture that allows for acknowledging power dynamics and historical inequities.
> 3. Focus on validating, not judging.
> 4. Follow through on your commitments to the relationship.

Co-coaching is about being a coach and a team member at the same time. We coach and we receive coaching simultaneously. It's a collaborative balance of suggesting and receiving, in which five contexts come into play, according to Kimsey-House, Kimsey-House, Sandahl, and Whitworth (2011):

- Listening
- Intuition
- Curiosity
- Momentum
- Self-Management

Those five contexts help us build relationships, based on trust. Let's think for a moment about a team working together to build a structure of some sort. It might be a two-person team building a small structure, such as a garden shed. Or it might be a large team, raising a barn. In both cases, team members lead and are led, based on curiosity and intuition. They need to listen to one another and manage themselves to get the job done well. You might wonder: What am I building in my classroom or school? Well, the answer comes from within you. You are building whatever you have pinpointed as needing to be changed to improve literacy practices for your students.

LISTENING

This is from Leo Buscaglia's poem "Listen":

> Listen! All I ask is that you listen.
> Don't talk or do—just hear me…
> And I can do for myself; I am not helpless.
> Maybe discouraged and faltering,
> but not helpless.

Listening is about hearing—truly hearing—what the other person is saying. When we listen well, we settle in and pay attention to the person sharing.

Listening is about hearing—truly hearing—what the other person is saying. When we listen well, we settle in and pay attention to the person sharing. We don't think about what we are going to say, or what advice we are going to give (Rosenberg, 2015). If you allow yourself to listen, your colleague is more likely to find her own answer in her thoughts. Finding our own answers to what troubles us about our instruction, with the support of a colleague, is freeing.

When we listen, we reflect on what a person says. For instance, if you are working with your colleague on incorporating more discussion into shared reading, and an attempt at that didn't go well for your colleague, you might reflect and then say, "I hear you saying that during the shared reading you usually don't give wait time, but when you paused, the students didn't say anything. That made you feel unsure of yourself." Or we can listen for something beneath the surface of what the person is saying. For example, Carly was talking with me about her struggle to increase the amount of time she devotes to independent reading. Here is a snippet of conversation.

What Carly and I Said	Why I Said What I Said
Carly: "I can't do independent reading every day."	
Me: "Tell me more about that."	To encourage more detail
Carly: "My students get really distracted, and they don't read for more than five to seven minutes. It just doesn't work to expect more."	
Me: "What do they do during the five to seven minutes?"	To get a clearer picture of what is happening in her classroom
Carly: "They have their one book from the library and they read, then the hum of voices begins at about the 5-minute mark. It happens even if I use a visual timer. I just have a small library and I am really frustrated."	
Me: "I am wondering if the students need more reading options."	To suggest an idea
Carly: "Yes, that's it. I don't have enough books and it makes me mad that the school just bought a new copy machine for the first wing."	
Me: "Oh, yes. Well, it sounds like you are wishing some money could have been spent on classroom libraries."	To confirm and validate Carly's feelings

In this conversation, I did four things. First, I listened. Second, I asked Carly to elaborate so that I could visualize what was happening in her classroom. Third, I resisted interjecting what was happening in my classroom; I stayed focused on Carly. And fourth, I suggested what she might be feeling.

INTUITION

Intuition is listening closely, below the surface of what the person is saying (Kimsey-House, Kimsey-House, Sandahl, & Whitworth, 2011), and I used it in my conversation with Carly. Your colleague is not going to tell you his deepest thoughts and feelings. But when you listen closely, using intuition, you can tease them out and truly hear the message.

Our own experiences teaching literacy and participating in the literacy walks ensure shared understandings with our colleagues. We will intuitively know about some of the things we are working on together, as well as about what the debrief meeting reveals when it comes to reaching our team goal. We can combine our personal knowledge gained from those experiences with what our colleagues say, and then apply our intuition to tease out more insights and ideas. We can dig into our learning needs and the learning needs of our students. From there, we can outline a plan to work together and support one another and our students.

CURIOSITY

Good listeners are curious. Within themselves, they have solutions to their problems, but often cannot find them on their own. They need a friend to help them discover what they already know. It's much like Dorothy in *The Wizard of Oz*, who always had a way to get home, but couldn't find it within herself until her traveling companions helped her. We can do this for each other in co-coaching relationships.

How do we develop curiosity when coaching one another? We ask questions— good questions that lead to self-discovery. Be open, playful, and thoughtful. Ask your colleague to describe what she was thinking, feeling, seeing, and hearing during instruction to reveal what is truly going on in the classroom. By doing that, you pinpoint what she might do next in her own learning and her students' learning.

How do we develop curiosity when coaching one another? We ask questions—good questions that lead to self-discovery. Be open, playful, and thoughtful.

MOMENTUM

Coaching is about continuing to learn (Knight, 2018) and maintaining the momentum to learn. When we learn in teams, we share experiences that help us move forward in our teaching. We deepen our learning about our teaching and our students' learning. The focus of coaching should not be limited to action. It should also be about evolving in our understanding of our instruction and how our instruction impacts students, both academically and emotionally.

Moving forward is the opposite of being stuck. Whenever I pull out my smartphone in a traffic jam and use an app to find an alternative route, my friend laughs at me because it can take me just as long to get where I am going because the alternative route is longer. But I tell her, "It feels so good to just keep moving!" Like being stuck in traffic, we can sometimes get stuck in our teaching practices.

When that happens, the first thing to do is talk with your colleagues about what is going on in your classroom, how you're feeling about it, and whether you're afraid of something. Fear often keeps us from moving forward. Sometimes that fear may be rooted in appearing incompetent or in losing control of your class. Other times it may be rooted in beliefs that are not serving student learning. Regardless of what's causing the fear, it helps to have a colleague guide you through a conversation, asking questions to figure out answers.

Too often teachers are pressured to focus on results. It might feel dissolute to think about how to keep your momentum going while learning new teaching strategies to understand our instruction. But maintaining momentum in a coaching relationship is not about looking at data-driven decisions; it is about developing understanding of how to become better at instruction (Knight, 2018). In Chapter 9 I present several literacy walk Reflection Sheets designed to help you focus on what students can do so that you can pinpoint their struggles and triumphs. Knowing the instructional impetus for those struggles and triumphs can be very helpful. I don't mean to imply that all student struggles and triumphs are the result of our efforts. After all, students are complex and many factors affect their learning. But research shows that the teacher's actions are the number-one factor of influence on student learning (Darling-Hammond & Oakes, 2019).

Let's take a look at how that conversation with Carly helped her keep momentum.

What Carly and I Said	Why I Said What I Said
I left off with me saying: "Oh, yes. Well, it sounds like you are wishing some money could have been spent on classroom libraries."	To let Carly know that I heard her wishes and desires. I wanted to validate Carly.
Me: "What would having more books do for you?"	To express my curiosity about how Carly would use the books. I wanted Carly to brainstorm possible usage she had not thought of.
Carly: "Well, it isn't just having more books, it is about the type of books. I want students to see themselves in the books. I want books in my classroom library that represent my students' ethnicities and races."	To listen carefully and thoughtfully to Carly

What Carly and I Said	Why I Said What I Said
Me: "It sounds like this is important to you."	To get at Carly's motivation
Carly: "Yes, it is. I was reading about how having a diverse collection of books not only validates students' lived experiences, it increases student motivation to read. They can hopefully relate to what is happening in books as well and make connections."	To listen and reflect on Carly's thinking
Me: "I hear you saying you want students to make text connections. How could this help you with your instruction?"	To encourage Carly to go deeper into what having a diverse collection of books can do for her classroom culture and instruction
Carly: "I am afraid that if all my books are about white people, my students of color will think they are not valued. It is like a subliminal message."	To listen to Carly. I wanted Carly to be bolder and to let go of old thinking or stereotyping. However, I knew lecturing would not help, so I asked another question.
Me: "Do you think being valued helps students make connections when reading?"	To urge Carly to deepen her thinking about what a diverse set of books can do for her students and for her classroom culture, rather than leading her thinking.
Carly: "Yes. I really do. Sometimes when I ask my Black students what they think a character is thinking or feeling, I know my library has mostly white people depicted in the book doing white, middle-class things. I am asking a Black child to relate themselves to whiteness. I should have books students can read that they see their own experiences in and which celebrates them for being Black. This is just wrong of me to do this."	To listen to Carly to reinforce her and her thinking
Me: "I hear you saying that you believe you are affecting students' sense of self by what you have available for them to read. And this affects their comprehension?"	To help Carly connect the dots in her thinking about the richness of the diverse library and the student comprehension she longs for. I am trying to get out of the way and let Carly feel what she is feeling and thinking. If she doesn't make the connection right now, that is okay, she might later on.
Carly: "I hadn't thought about it that way before, but yes, when my students connect with what they're reading, they're going to stay engaged and get much more out of their reading."	

SELF-MANAGEMENT

In a co-coaching conversation, the best thing we can do when a colleague shares is get out of the way. We need to set aside our egos, thoughts, feelings, and opinions. When we are coaching each other, and it is your turn to listen, the one who's speaking should be in the spotlight, which may require some self-management on your part. You need to hold your tongue and *listen* and do your best to suspend judgment because it is essential to being part of a community of practice (Pascual-Leone & Greenberg, 2007). It is vital to being a good team member during literacy walks and a good co-coach afterwards. Focus on the team.

Encouraging Reflection in Co-Coaching

Literacy walks are about learning and growing as a team, and that's just what you're doing when you co-coach with colleagues: helping one another learn and grow as a team. In addition to speaking and listening to one another about teaching practices, you can also reflect together. By reflecting together, you think deeply about what you're learning and, therefore, are more likely to design the best environments for you to thrive as professionals and for your students to grow as learners. There are many processes to help you get the most out of reflecting together (Curedale, 2017). Three particularly useful processes during co-coaching are constructive feedback, Benefit Maps, and Empathy Maps.

CONSTRUCTIVE FEEDBACK

Constructive feedback requires using the five constructs of co-coaching (listening, intuition, curiosity, momentum, and self-management) and, therefore, helps you to identify and understand problems with your implementation of literacy practices and to brainstorm solutions. The goal of the constructive feedback process is to develop skills in giving and receiving input effectively (Curedale, 2017). When all team members can give and receive feedback thoughtfully and carefully, they can build on the team's ideas and individual team member's ideas.

The Constructive Feedback Process	
Goal	To develop skills in giving and receiving constructive feedback so that the ideas of the team and team members can be developed collectively
Participants	A group of five to six teachers
Steps	1. Using the literacy walk Reflection Sheets from Chapter 9, choose a focus area and have team members discuss (practice listening) their personal thoughts about what they did during instruction, what worked well, and what could be improved upon. 2. Generate a few next-step actions related to the thoughts and perceptions from the discussion about the implementation of comprehensive literacy practices and write them on sticky notes. This is about six or more sticky notes per person with one notation on each sticky note. Place the sticky notes where everyone can see them. 3. Have each team member choose three possible next-step actions from the presented ideas. 4. Have each team member generate up to three positive things about his or her selected ideas, considering the needs of the team. Each member shares by saying words like "I notice…" and "I wonder…" in order to focus on "I" messages that don't detract from others' thoughts and ideas. 5. Ask a team member to write the suggestion on a whiteboard or chart paper. 6. Have the team select the three most preferred ideas for next steps and brainstorm how they could support each other in implementing the ideas.

BENEFIT MAPS

Benefit Maps help the team decide on next-step actions—individual actions, not collective ones. During the Benefit Map process, each person assigns relative importance and weight to ideas they are considering based on the literacy walk Reflection Sheets from Chapter 9. This map can help teachers communicate their ideas and discuss their choices with team members. It helps build communication.

The Benefit Map Process	
Goal	To decide on which next steps to focus on for maximum benefit
Participants	A group of two to six teachers
Steps	1. Explain the Benefit Map to the team and tell members they are going to work through one together. Afterward, each member will complete his or her own Benefit Map. 2. Using the literacy walk Reflection Sheets from Chapter 9, have each team member note five to six next-step actions he or she is considering. 3. Using the Benefit Map template (on page 156 and at scholastic.com/ LiteracyWalksResources), place each next-step action in one of the quadrants of the map, ranking them based on the axes of the four quadrants (high benefit-easy to implement; high benefit-hard to implement; less benefit-easy to implement; less benefit-hard to implement). 4. Have team members debrief and share their maps and decide on two actions that they want to take based on their axis ranking.

Benefit Map

High Benefit

Using a sound wall to help students see the letters that make up the sounds.

Singing more songs in the classroom that have rhyming words to give students opportunities to play with sounds.

Putting a sound wall up near my teaching area.

Learning all of the parts of our new reading program, especially the phonemic-awareness components.

Sending sound books home each week for students to read at home. (It takes a lot of copies.)

Easy to Implement

Hard to Implement

While of great benefit to teachers, collaborative planning of phonemic-awareness lessons won't directly impact student learning if we don't follow through with teaching the lessons.

Buying and storing small items and manipulatives that represent the sounds. For example, toy elephants, apples, or trucks.

Low Benefit

EMPATHY MAPS

Empathy Maps help team members share their personal experiences about literacy practices they're implementing. The purpose is for members to understand one another's thoughts and feelings about those experiences, whether good or bad (Curedale, 2017). In a co-coaching relationship, it is important to honor each other's thoughts and feelings about how implementation is going—something that rarely happens in a typical day because teachers are encouraged to push thoughts and feelings aside. Hall and Hord (2019) point out that, in the process of learning, we go through a series of thoughts and feelings. As co-coaches work together, they can help each other work through their thoughts and feelings so they don't become discouraged or angry, and instead keep moving forward. When a colleague understands our situation and listens to our thoughts and feelings, our instruction improves.

The Empathy Map Process	
Goal	To decide on next steps to focus on for maximum benefit
Participants	A group of two to three teachers, working together on a map
Steps	1. In the circle in the middle of the Empathy Map template (on page 157 and at scholastic.com/LiteracyWalksResources), write the name and grade level or teaching position of the team. The radial boxes around the circle represent the team's experience implementing instructional practices.
	2. Have team members encourage the focus person to talk about what she or he sees and does during a lesson. It is important that the person share what she actually does, not what she is expected to do, so that members can understand her experiences. Write the thoughts expressed in the "say/do" box.
	3. Have the focus person describe what he or she hears and sees during the lesson. This can be what he or she sees and then what he or she typically hears students say. The idea is to convey the teaching experience in a way that allows it to be visualized. Write the thoughts expressed in the "see/hear" boxes.
	4. Have the focus person share how he or she thinks and feels while teaching the lessons, and write what he or she says in the "think/feel" box.
	5. Have team members, using their intuition, describe the difficulties that the focus person seems to be having and list them below the radial boxes. The point of doing this is to validate the person and let him or her know that the team empathizes. Talking openly about what is difficult can be freeing because, as teachers, we are alone during instruction and don't always have the time or space to talk with colleagues about difficult or less-than-perfect moments.
	6. Have team members ask the focus person questions about what he or she feels is positive about the teaching, what he or she is gaining from the teaching, and what students are gaining from it. Members then encourage the person to set a goal for him- or herself after considering the pains and gains listed. Essentially, team members ask the person, "What could be your next step?"

Empathy Map

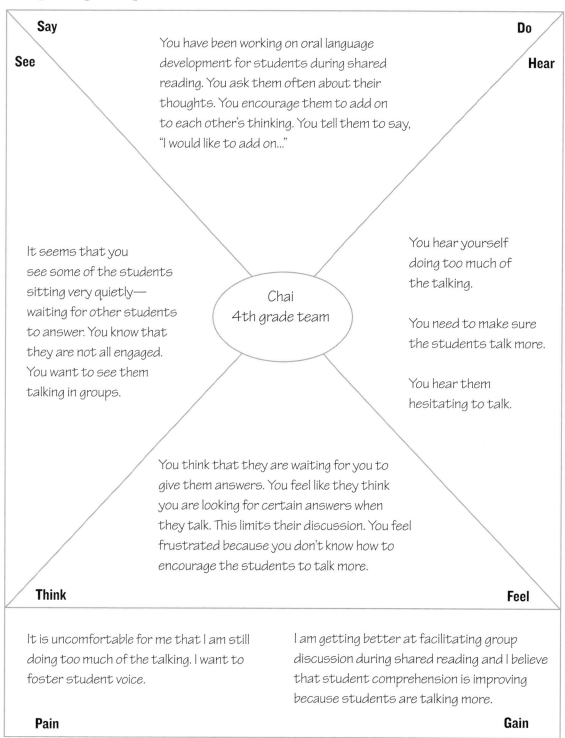

Say / **See**

You have been working on oral language development for students during shared reading. You ask them often about their thoughts. You encourage them to add on to each other's thinking. You tell them to say, "I would like to add on..."

Do / **Hear**

It seems that you see some of the students sitting very quietly— waiting for other students to answer. You know that they are not all engaged. You want to see them talking in groups.

Chai
4th grade team

You hear yourself doing too much of the talking.

You need to make sure the students talk more.

You hear them hesitating to talk.

You think that they are waiting for you to give them answers. You feel like they think you are looking for certain answers when they talk. This limits their discussion. You feel frustrated because you don't know how to encourage the students to talk more.

Think / **Feel**

Pain

It is uncomfortable for me that I am still doing too much of the talking. I want to foster student voice.

Gain

I am getting better at facilitating group discussion during shared reading and I believe that student comprehension is improving because students are talking more.

Bringing It All Together

Co-coaching is rewarding. First, it builds collegiality. As you develop trust with one another, you deepen your relationship and engage in powerful, constructive conversations. Second, co-coaching gives you power. You and your teammates are leading your own professional growth and development. In this chapter, I provided several ways to work together through co-coaching—suggestions to keep you moving forward.

So get started with co-coaching! Approach a colleague and talk about working with one another. Don't be afraid to be authentic and show your vulnerability. You will develop strong co-coaching bonds if you are open and honest from the start. Remember, there is no perfect teaching, and we don't work together to be perfect. We work together to grow.

CHAPTER 9

Recording What's Working
Coach and Teacher Reflect

"I know we need some professional development on how to rev up student engagement during shared reading, but I am struggling with understanding what my actions need to be, exactly. If I could visualize myself in action, I think it would be so much more powerful for me to know what best practices I need to implement."

—CHARLENE, EIGHTH-GRADE TEACHER

We use student-facing Data-Collection Tools on literacy walks because it is important to focus squarely on what and how students are learning, in addition to what and how the teacher is teaching. However, when working with a coach, that's not necessarily the case. This chapter is about taking a look at your practices and using Reflection Sheets to gather thoughts and guide conversations.

Reflecting on Teaching Practices

The Reflection Sheets in this chapter are *not* intended to be used as Data-Collection Tools, but rather tools for individual teachers to use *after* a literacy walk, once the debrief meeting is complete, and a teacher and coach are working together. I have learned from offering professional development across the country (and world) that it's important for teachers to focus on their own growth as individuals. It is about their learning, their personal growth. Brené Brown (2015) says that vulnerability is "the willingness to show up and be seen with no guarantee of outcome" (p. xvii). I really believe that. If you are to stretch in your practice, you must allow yourself to be vulnerable. The sheets in this chapter are designed to give you direction, and, like buoys in the deep water, ensure your safety.

When we reflect on our practices, we can better align our goals to our outcomes (Darling-Hammond, Hyler, & Gardner, 2017). For instance, I might set a goal of engaging students at least eight times during an interactive read-aloud, but after the read-aloud, I realize I answered my own questions, and students didn't do much talking. So, if my goal was to engage students a minimum of eight times, but my outcome was loads of teacher talk and minimal student talk, I clearly need to reflect on my practice to see what I could be doing differently. The Reflection Sheets help us first think through what our instruction should look like, and then note what we actually do and what, if anything, we need to change or improve.

The sheets in the appendix, pages 141–155, and at scholastic.com/LiteracyWalksResources, will help you reflect on your instruction of key literacy practices.

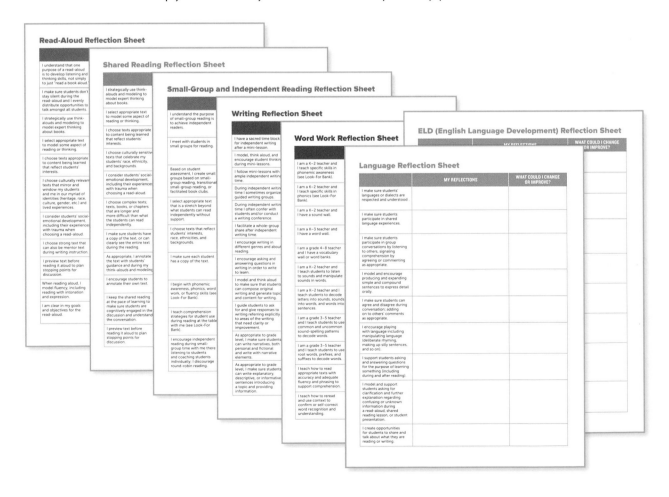

You will also find online a blank, customizable Reflection Sheet so you can create your own focus and list of actions and strategies. Think of each essential element as a file drawer. Each drawer can be pulled out and dug into for more specifics in practice and refinement. These sheets list the basic actions you would take to align your instructional practices with student outcomes; they are not designed to list every action you could possibly take to ensure learning.

CREATING A PLAYBOOK

The Reflection Sheets act as a playbook to help you plan instruction in order to reach the outcomes you desire. You might think about and write down what you want to change or improve as your objectives. When you write down your thoughts, you are more likely to remember them!

Think of outcomes in terms of what the students are doing to learn. For instance, if I facilitate a lesson in a way that encourages students to preview a book or text on their own before reading, and then the students do that independently, with or without my prompting, I know that I am on the road to success when it comes to that strategy. On the other hand, if I teach the lesson again, and the students are unable to apply the strategy without extreme levels of scaffolding from me, I'll need to revisit my instruction. If I provide time and support for guided practice, then I know that the students will have an opportunity to do the work for themselves, rather than watching me or listening to me the whole time.

A playbook is a series of actions and strategies that you plan to take to implement your teaching moves. Those actions and strategies can come from your literacy objectives. You might also reflect on how you are doing with following the gradual release of responsibility model by balancing shared, guided, and independent instruction. Ultimately, make sure you offer purposeful and authentic tasks to ensure that students are engaged. What you plan can become a roadmap for your personal journey.

> The Reflection Sheets help us first think through what our instruction should look like, and then note what we actually do and what, if anything, we need to change or improve.

See the Read-Aloud Reflection Sheet below, which was filled out by a teacher during a coaching session I conducted. He added notes next to each guideline about what he remembered doing during the lesson and how it went. These are his reflective notes. In the column on the right, he then listed a couple of notes about what he wanted to work on.

Read-Aloud Reflection Sheet

	MY REFLECTIONS	WHAT COULD I CHANGE OR IMPROVE?
I understand that one purpose of a read-aloud is to develop listening and thinking skills, not simply to just "read a book aloud."	I really feel I understand this now.	I could have students pair-share first.
I make sure students don't stay silent during the read-aloud and I evenly distribute opportunities to talk amongst all students.	I am working on this. Some of my students are really shy and don't like to talk in the group.	Plan out how I would implement.
I strategically use think-alouds and modeling to model expert thinking about books.	I have been stopping and sharing my thinking, hoping to provide an example of how to talk about books and ideas.	
I select appropriate text to model some aspect of reading or thinking.	I am still having trouble figuring out which book is best for which strategy I want to teach.	I could ask my colleagues what books they use for modeling certain strategies.
I choose texts appropriate to content being learned that reflect students' interests.	I feel good about ensuring my students are excited about the books that we are reading.	
I choose culturally relevant texts that mirror and window my students and me in our myriad of identities (heritage, race, culture, gender, etc.) and lived experiences.	I have been careful to have an array of culturally responsive books in the classroom where students can see themselves and others different from themselves.	
I consider students' social-emotional development, including their experiences with trauma when choosing a read-aloud.	I have not yet begun to focus on this yet, I need to get better at using the right book with the right strategy first.	I could look for books that work in reading and writing.
I choose strong text that can also be mentor text during writing instruction.	I am getting better at this, but sometimes I am choosing a book only to model reading strategies.	
I preview text before reading it aloud to plan stopping points for discussion.	I have been getting better about this. I find that when I don't preplan, the lesson does not go as well. When I preplan the stopping points—finding powerful places—students have more to say.	I need to continue to plan and add tabs to the text so I remember to stop in the right spot.
When reading aloud, I model fluency, including reading with intonation and expression.	I am good at this. I like reading aloud to the students.	
I am clear in my goals and objectives for the read-aloud.	I am not always clear about what I want to accomplish. Sometimes I want students to just enjoy the book, but they are more engaged when we stop and discuss.	I can preplan places to stop where there are powerful ideas.

Read-Aloud Reflection Sheet *continued*

	MY REFLECTIONS	WHAT COULD I CHANGE OR IMPROVE?
I explicitly model, as appropriate, my goals for instruction in fluency appropriate to my grade level (see the Look-For Bank).	I am getting better at this but I still need practice!	I can set one goal per week to make sure I am focusing on fluency as well as comprehension strategies.
I discuss and model the goals for comprehension instruction appropriate to my grade level (see the Look-For Bank).	Yes. I feel good about this. I am good at modeling.	
I am a teacher in grades K–2 and I stop reading from time to time and ask who, what, why, when, where, and how questions.		
I am a teacher in grades 3–8 and I stop reading from time to time to ask deep comprehension questions (see the Look-For Bank).	I feel good about the questions I am asking.	I need to improve how much time I am giving for wait time to allow my students to think before responding.
During text discussion, I am a facilitator; students do the majority of the talking.	Well, this is HARD. I am talking too much.	I could encourage students to jot notes so they can remember what they want to say.
I stop and think aloud about confusing points or misunderstandings about the text.	I am doing this fairly well. This is part of the problem. I focus on asking them too many low-level questions and we don't have deep discussions about the text.	
I stop and discuss unknown or confusing vocabulary and encourage students to make inferences to understand word meaning.	I need to work on this! I think I don't do this well, I forget that the students may not know all the vocabulary words.	I could preteach vocabulary words.
I make sure students are speaking audibly and with independence.	I am going to worry about this later in the year—right now I am thrilled if they are talking and sharing.	
I facilitate collaborative conversations about text, story, and nonfiction topics.	This is my overall goal!	I will check myself next month and see if I am improving at this.

References: Easley, 2004

Bringing It All Together

We transform our practices through continual reflection and adjustments to our teaching. When we reflect, we self-direct our learning and discover so much about our students' learning. Being open to what is happening in the classroom enables us to see the current reality and set goals. We cannot transform our classrooms without reflecting on our instruction and reflecting on what *we are actually doing,* not what we had planned to do or hoped to do. The Reflection Sheets can help you identify your current reality and take steps to move forward.

References

Akhavan, N. L. (2011). *The effects of coaching on teacher efficacy, individual academic optimism, and student achievement.* ProQuest.

Aguilar, E. (2013). *The art of coaching: Effective strategies for school transformation.* Wiley.

Bandura, A (1977). Self-efficacy: Toward a unifying theory of behavioral change. *Psychological Review. 84*(2): 191–215.

Bens, I. (2005). *Facilitating with ease! Core skills for facilitators, team leaders and members, managers, consultants, and trainers.* Jossey-Bass.

Bernhardt, V. L. (2017). *Data analysis for continuous school improvement.* Routledge.

Boudette, R. J. K. P., City, E. A., & Murnane, R. J. (2013). *Data wise: A step-by-step guide to using assessment results to improve teaching and learning.* Harvard Education Press.

Brockett, R. G. (1994). Resistance to self-direction in adult learning: Myths and misunderstandings. *New Directions for Adult and Continuing Education, 64,* 5–12.

Brockett, R. G., & Hiemstra, R. (2018). *Self-direction in adult learning: Perspectives in theory, research and practice.* Routledge.

Brooks, R., Brooks, S., & Goldstein, S. (2012). The power of mindsets: Nurturing engagement, motivation, and resilience in students. In S. L. Christenson, A. L. Reschly, & C. Wylie (Eds.), *Handbook of research on student engagement* (pp. 541–562). Springer Science + Business Media. https://doi.org/10.1007/978-1-4614-2018-7_26

Brown, B. (2010). *The gifts of imperfection: Let go of who you think you are supposed to be and embrace who you are.* Hazelden Publishing.

Brown, B. (2015). *Rising strong.* Spiegel & Grau.

Brown, P. C., Roediger III, M. L., & McDaniel, M. A. (2014). *Make it stick: The science of successful learning.* The Belknap Press of Harvard University.

Bryk, A., & Schneider, B. (2002). *Trust in schools: A core resource for improvement.* Russell Sage Foundation.

Bryk, A., Gomez, L. M., Grunow, A., & LeMathieu, P. G. (2015). *Learning to improve: How America's schools can get better at getting better.* Harvard Education Press.

City, E. A., Elmore, R. F., Fiarman, S. E., & Teitel, L. (2009). *Instructional rounds in education: A network approach to improving teaching and learning.* Harvard Education Press.

Curedale, R. A. (2017). *Design thinking: Process and methods guide, 4th edition.* Design Community College.

Curtis, R. E., & City, E. A. (2009). *Strategy in action: How schools can support powerful teaching and learning.* Harvard Education Press.

Darling-Hammond, L., & Oakes, J. (2019). *Preparing teachers for deeper learning.* Harvard Education Press.

Darling-Hammond, L., Hyler, M. E., & Gardner, M. (2017). Effective teacher professional development. Palo Alto, CA: Learning Policy Institute. Retrieved from: https://learningpolicyinstitute.org/sites/default/files/product-files/Effective_Teacher_Professional_Development_REPORT.pdf

Dweck, C. S. (2007). *Mindset: The new psychology of success.* Ballantine Books.

Elmore, R. F., & City, E. A. (2007). The road to school improvement. In Walser, N. & Chauncey, C. (Eds.), *Spotlight on leadership and school change.* Harvard Education Press. Also in (2007, May/June). Harvard Education Letter, 23(3)

Emerson, R. M., Fretz, R. I., & Shaw, L. I. (2011). *Writing ethnographic field notes, second edition.* The University of Chicago Press.

Fergus, E. A. (2016). *Solving disproportionality and achieving equity: A leader's guide to using data to change hearts and minds.* Corwin Press.

Fullan, M., & Quinn, J. (2016). *Coherence: The right drivers in action for schools, districts, and systems.* Ontario Principals' Council and Corwin Press.

Fuller, F. F. (1969). Concerns of teachers: A developmental conceptualization. *American Educational Research Journal 6*(2), 207–226.

Fritz, R. (1999). *The path of least resistance for managers.* Fawcett Books.

Goree, J., & Akhavan, N. (in press). Middle school students' needs for effective reading comprehension strategies in the classroom focused on 21st century learning skills. In Main, K., & Whatman, S. (Eds.) *Health and well-being in the middle grades: Research for effective middle level education.* IAP/Information Age Publishing.

Hall, G. E., & Hord, S. M. (2019). *Implementing change: Patterns, principles, and potholes,* fifth edition. Pearson.

Hargrove, R. (2008) *Masterful coaching,* third edition. Pfeiffer.

Harvey, M. (2015). *Interactional leadership and how to coach it: The art of the choice-focused leader.* Routledge.

Hattie, J. (2008). *Visible learning: A synthesis of over 800 meta-analyses relating to achievement.* Routledge.

Horn, I. S., & Little, J. W. (2010). Attending to Problems of Practice: Routines and Resources for Professional Learning in Teachers' Workplace Interactions. *American Educational Research Journal 47*(1), 181–217.

Husband, T., & Kang, G. (2020). Identifying Promising Literacy Practices for Black Males in P–12 Classrooms: An Integrative Review. *Journal of Language and Literacy Education, 16*(1).

Johnston, J., Dozier, C., & Smit, J. (2016). How language supports adaptive teaching through a responsive learning culture. *Reading Psychology, 41*(2), 71–86.

Kaplan, A., & Maehr, M. L. (2007). The Contributions and Prospects of Goal Orientation Theory. *Educational Psychology Review, 19,* 141–184.

Kearsley, G. (2010). Andragogy (M. Knowles). The Theory Into Practice database. Retrieved from http://tip.psychology.org

Kelcey, B., & Carlisle, J. F. (2013). Learning about teachers' literacy instruction from classroom observations. *Reading Research Quarterly, 3,* 301–317.

Kimsey-House, H., Kimsey-House, K., Sandahl, P., & Whitworth, L. (2011). *Co-Active coaching: Changing business, transforming lives.* Nicholas Brealey Publications.

Knight, J. (2018). *The impact cycle: What instructional coaches should do to foster powerful improvements in teaching.* Corwin.

Knowles, M. (1984). *The adult learner: A neglected species,* third edition. Gulf Publishing.

Kosanovich, M., Smith, K., Hensley, T., Osborne-Lampkin, L., & Foorman, B. (2015). *School leader's literacy walkthrough: Kindergarten, first, second, and third grades.* Regional Educational Laboratory Southeast.

Langer, J. L., & Moldoveanu, M. (2000). The construct of mindfulness. *Journal of Social Issues, 56*(1), 1–9.

Law, H. (2013). *The psychology of coaching, mentoring and learning.* Wiley-Blackwell.

Mierink, J., Imants, J. Mejier, P. C., & Verloop, N. (2010). Teacher learning and collaboration in innovative teams. *Cambridge Journal of Education, 40*(2), 161–181.

Moss, C. M., & Brookhart, S. M. (2015). *Formative classroom walkthroughs: How principals and teachers collaborate to raise student achievement.* ASCD.

Ogunyemi, D. C., Clare, Y., Astudillo, Y. M., Marseille, M., Manu, E., & Kim, S. (2020). Microaggressions in the learning environment: A systematic review. *Journal of Diversity in Higher Education, 13*(2), 97–119.

Rosenberg, M. B. (2015). *Nonviolent communication: A language of life.* Puddle Dancer Press.

Saphier, J., Haley-Speca, M. A., & Gower, R. (2008). *The skillful teacher: Building your teaching skills,* sixth edition. Research for Better Teaching, Inc. Schwandt.

Senge, P. M. (1990). *The fifth discipline: The art & practice of the learning organization.* Doubleday Business.

Stake, R. E. (1995). *The art of case study research.* Sage Publications.

Stake, R. E. (2005). Qualitative Case Studies. In N. K. Denzin & Y. S. Lincoln (Eds.), *The Sage handbook of qualitative research* (p. 443–466). Sage Publications Ltd.

Stroh, D. P., & Zurcher, K. (2020, May 4). *Acting and thinking systematically.* The Systems Thinker. https://thesystemsthinker.com/acting-and-thinking-systemically/

Taylor, R., & Chanter, C. (2019). *The coaching partnership: Collaboration for systemic change.* Scholastic.

Tschannen-Moran, M. (2004). Fostering student learning: The relationship of collective teacher efficacy and student achievement. *Leadership and Policy in Schools 3*(3), 189–209.

Appendix

For instructions on how to use the Data-Collection Tool Template and the Look-For Banks, see Chapter 5 (pages 40–55). For instructions on how to use the Reflection Sheets, see Chapter 9 (pages 89–93). All appendix items can be downloaded at scholastic.com/ LiteracyWalksResources.

Data-Collection Tool

Team Goal:		
Grade(s):	Teacher(s):	Date(s):

Component(s) to Observe:	☐ Read-Aloud ☐ Shared Reading ☐ Small-Group and Independent Reading ☐ Word Work ☐ Writing ☐ Language	
Classroom Arrangement:	☐ Whole-Class ☐ Small Group ☐ Individual	

LOOK-FORS BY CATEGORY	TEACHER SAYS/DOES	STUDENTS SAY/DO
[Paste by category look-fors from the bank for your chosen component(s) here.]		

Data-Collection Tool

LOOK-FORS BY CATEGORY	TEACHER SAYS/DOES	STUDENTS SAY/DO
[Paste by category look-fors from the bank for your chosen component(s) here.]		

Look-For Banks

Read-Aloud • Look-For Bank

LOOK-FOR CATEGORIES	KINDERGARTEN	GRADE 1	GRADE 2
Environment	• Complex and engaging text is used for read-aloud (i.e., texts that have multiple levels of meaning appropriate for the grade level and contain complex and/or multiple themes and language that is not too simple). There is a balance between fiction and nonfiction. • The classroom library is large and contains an extensive range of topics, text types, and genres. • The classroom is filled with books and other texts on a variety of topics and in a variety of genres, and reflect students' races, cultures, and identities.		• The classroom is vibrant, with students and teacher listening to and speaking with one another about texts and information. • Anchor charts are posted around the room that capture collaborative efforts from literacy lessons.
Print Concepts	• Understand parts of the book. • Understand the roles of the author and illustrator.		
Fluency	• Are exposed to fluent oral reading (e.g., phrasing and expression).		
Comprehension	• Teacher points out and clarifies new vocabulary words.		
	• Recognize genre and genre features. • Ask and answer questions about the text. • Describe the illustrations and the meaning illustrations provide to the text. • Identify main topic and key details in nonfiction texts.		
	• Recognize and discuss beginnings, middle details, and endings in fiction texts. • Discuss characters and character experiences, thoughts, and feelings. • Compare and contrast the adventures of characters in familiar stories. • Discuss how details support important points in nonfiction text; identify the author's purpose for writing the text. • Discuss new words in group discussion.	• Retell the story, including key details, and discuss the central message or theme of the story. • Identify who is telling the story. • Identify author point of view and, for nonfiction, the author's purpose for writing the text. • Describe connections between individuals, ideas, events, and information in a text. • Make predictions about what will happen in the story based on text details and prior knowledge.	
		• Describe characters, settings, and major events in the story, noting details. • Listen to and discuss a book or chapter that is longer and more difficult than a book or chapter that can be read independently or with assistance. • Distinguish between books that tell stories and books that give information.	• Ask and answer *who, what, why, when,* and *where* questions to demonstrate understanding of the text. • Use details to describe how characters respond to major events in the story. • Describe plot, noting how details in the beginning and middle lead to the ending. • Acknowledge differences in point of view of characters, including speaking in a different voice when reading aloud.

Read-Aloud • Look-For Bank

LOOK-FOR CATEGORIES	KINDERGARTEN	GRADE 1	GRADE 2
Comprehension (cont.)			• Compare and contrast two versions of the same story. • Identify main topic and key details of multi-paragraph nonfiction texts, as well as the topic of individual paragraphs. • Use information from words and pictures to describe characters, setting, and plot. • Use text features in nonfiction text (e.g., diagrams, photographs) to understand main points. • Compare and contrast stories and texts on the same subject or topic. • Describe connections between events, ideas, or concepts in nonfiction texts, including historical, scientific, and procedural texts. • Point out and clarify new vocabulary words. • Use text features in nonfiction text to locate key facts or information. • Describe how reasons support the author's point(s). • Think through earlier predictions and why they were or were not correct, referring to the text for details.
Engagement	• Are central to the discussion, and do the majority of thinking and talking about texts. • Speak audibly and independently. • Teacher discusses confusing points or misunderstandings about the text. • Teacher discusses words regularly and posts them around the room. • Teacher discusses new or confusing vocabulary words and encourages inferences. • Teacher stops at points in the book to check students' listening comprehension, focusing on *who, what, why, when,* and *where* questions. • Teacher stops at points in the book to ask inquiry questions or deep comprehension questions. • Teacher encourages talk and responds to what students are saying, rather than correcting how they are saying it.		

Read-Aloud • Look-For Bank

LOOK-FOR CATEGORIES	GRADE 3	GRADE 4	GRADE 5
Environment	• The classroom is vibrant, with students and teacher listening to and speaking with one another about texts and information. • Anchor charts are posted around the room that capture collaborative efforts from literacy lessons.		
Fluency	• Are exposed to fluent oral reading (e.g., phrasing and expression).		
Comprehension	• Make predictions about what will happen in the story based on text details and prior knowledge. • Describe how reasons support the author's point(s). • Think through earlier predictions and why they were or were not correct, referring to the text for details. • Identify the author's purpose for writing a nonfiction text.		
	• Determine the main idea of a text and explain how key details support it. • Distinguish their own point of view apart from the narrator's and characters' points of view.		
	• Describe how characters' traits and motives impact story events. • Recount stories, fables, folktales, and myths from diverse cultures. • Ask questions about the text and explicitly refer to it to answer them. • Describe stories; determine central messages and identify them with details from the text. • Compare and contrast themes, settings, and plots of books in a series. • Describe the relationship between ideas, events, concepts, and information, using language that pertains to time, sequence, and cause/effect. • Use text features to locate information relevant to a given topic efficiently.	• Summarize the text using details and information drawn from it. • Determine themes in a story, drama, or poem from details in the text. • Draw inferences from a text, using details from text to support them. • Compare and contrast the treatment of similar themes and topics (e.g., good vs. evil) and patterns of events. • Explain events, procedures, ideas, or concepts in a historical, scientific, or technical text, including what happened and why, based on text details. • Interpret information presented visually, orally, or quantitatively (e.g., charts, graphs, timelines, diagrams, animations) and explain how the information contributes to an understanding of the text.	
		• Refer to details and examples in a text when explaining what it says explicitly. • Describe in depth a character (traits, thoughts, actions), setting, or event in a story or drama, drawing on specific details. • Compare and contrast the point of view from which different stories are narrated, including first and third person. • Explain structural differences between poetry, drama, and prose. • Explain how an author uses reasons and evidence to support points.	• Refer to details, examples, and quotes when explaining what the text says explicitly. • Describe how characters in a story respond to challenges. • Describe how the narrator of a poem reflects on a topic. • Compare and contrast characters (traits, thoughts, actions), in a story, drawing on specific details it contains. • Describe how the narrator's point of view influences descriptions of events. • Determine two or more main ideas in the text and explain how key details support them.

Read-Aloud • Look-For Bank

LOOK-FOR CATEGORIES	GRADE 3	GRADE 4	GRADE 5
Comprehension (cont.)		• Describe the structure (e.g., chronology, comparison, cause/effect, problem/solution) of events, ideas, concepts, or information in a nonfiction text or part of a text.	• Explain the relationships or interactions between two or more individuals, events, ideas, or concepts in a historical, scientific, or technical text, based on specific information it contains. • Integrate information from two texts on the same topic to write or speak about the topic knowledgeably. • Compare and contrast texts in the same genre or with similar themes and topics. • Analyze how a sentence, chapter, scene, or stanza helps to develop theme, setting, or plot. • Point out and clarify new vocabulary words and phrases, including domain-specific words, and literary techniques, including metaphors and similes. • Compare and contrast the overall structure (e.g., chronology, comparison, cause/effect, problem/solution) of events, ideas, concepts, or information in two or more texts. • Analyze multiple accounts of the same event or topic, noting important similarities and differences in the point of view they represent.
Engagement	• Are central to the discussion, and do the majority of thinking and talking about texts. • Speak audibly and independently. • Teacher discusses confusing points or misunderstandings about the text. • Teacher discusses words regularly and posts them around the room. • Teacher discusses new or confusing vocabulary words and encourages inferences. • Teacher stops at points in the book to check students' listening comprehension, focusing on *who, what, why, when,* and *where* questions. • Teacher stops at points in the book to ask inquiry questions or deep comprehension questions. • Teacher encourages talk and responds to what students are saying, rather than correcting how they are saying it.		

Read-Aloud • Look-For Bank

LOOK-FOR CATEGORIES	GRADE 6	GRADE 7	GRADE 8
Environment	• The classroom is vibrant, with students and teacher listening to and speaking with one another about texts and information. • Anchor charts are posted around the room that capture collaborative efforts from literacy lessons. • Words are discussed regularly and posted around the room. • Vocabulary wall is present, up-to-date, and filled with words students can use for reading and writing. • Student-written materials, charts, and other material display words and word meaning through words and drawings. • Talk is encouraged. Teacher responds to what students are saying rather than correcting how they are saying it. There is a balance of talk between students and teacher, where students are resources of information.		
Fluency	• Students are exposed to fluent oral reading (e.g., phrasing and expression).		
Comprehension	• Think through earlier predictions and why they did or did not come true, referring to the text explicitly for details.		
	• Analyze what a text says, citing evidence from it. • Determine a theme or central idea of a text and explain how it is conveyed through details. • Describe how a story or drama's plot unfolds in a series of episodes, as well as how the characters respond or change. • Explain how the author develops the narrator, character, or subject's point of view. • Determine the text's central idea and how it is conveyed through details. • Summarize texts objectively, without personal opinions. • Trace and evaluate a text for arguments and claims. • Compare and contrast one author's presentation of events with another's. • Analyze how a sentence, paragraph, chapter, or section fits into a text's overall structure and contributes to the development of the ideas. • Determine the meaning of a text's words and phrases, including figurative, connotative, and technical meanings.	• Cite several pieces of textual evidence which most strongly support an analysis of what the text says explicitly. • Draw inferences from the text using the most relevant details and quotes from text as support. • Determine multiple themes or central ideas in a text and analyze development of the theme or central idea throughout the text, including the relationship of the theme to characters, setting, and plot. • Analyze how particular lines of dialogue or incidents in a story propel the action, reveal aspects of character, or lead to a decision or turning point in the story. • Compare and contrast the structure of two or more texts, describing how the structure relates to meaning and style. • Analyze how differences in points of view of the characters in the story create effects such as suspense or humor. • Compare and contrast the fictional portrayal of a time, place, or character and a historical account of the same period as a means of understanding how authors of fiction use or alter history. • Analyze how modern fiction draws on traditional themes. • Determine the central idea of a nonfiction text and analyze its development through the text. • Summarize texts objectively without personal opinions. • Analyze in detail the structure of a specific paragraph, considering how the sentences in the paragraph define and refine a key concept. • Determine author's point of view or purpose for writing a text and analyze how the author acknowledges and responds to conflicting evidence or viewpoints. • Delineate and evaluate the argument and specific claims in a text, assessing whether the reasoning is sound and recognizing irrelevant evidence.	

Read-Aloud • Look-For Bank

LOOK-FOR CATEGORIES	GRADE 6	GRADE 7	GRADE 8
Comprehension (cont.)	• Make predictions about what will happen in the story, based on text details and prior knowledge. • Describe how reasons support the author's point(s). • Identify the author's purpose for writing a nonfiction text. • Draw inferences from a text, using details from the text to support them. • Compare and contrast the treatment of similar themes and topics (e.g., good vs. evil) and patterns of events. • Explain events, procedures, ideas, or concepts in a historical, scientific, or technical text, including what happened and why, based on text details. • Interpret information presented visually, orally, or quantitatively (e.g., charts, graphs, timelines, diagrams, animations) and explain how the information contributes to an understanding of the text. • Compare and contrast the overall structure (e.g., chronology, comparison, cause/effect, problem/solution) of events, ideas, concepts, or information in two or more texts. • Analyze multiple accounts of the same event or topic, noting important similarities and differences in the point of view they represent.	• Determine the meaning of words and phrases as they are used in a text, including analogies, allusions, and figurative, connotative, and technical meanings. • Analyze the impact of word choice on meaning and tone. • Compare and contrast the fictional portrayal of a time, place, or character and a historical account of the same period as a means of understanding how authors of fiction use or alter history. • Analyze how modern fiction draws on traditional themes.	

Read-Aloud • Look-For Bank

LOOK-FOR CATEGORIES	GRADE 6	GRADE 7	GRADE 8
Engagement	• Are central to the discussion, and do the majority of thinking and talking about texts.		
	• Speak audibly and independently.		
	• Teacher stops at points in the book to ask inquiry questions or deep comprehension questions.		
	• Teacher discusses confusing points or misunderstandings about the text.	• Teacher stops at points in the text to encourage students to build up a big idea about the text and share their thinking.	
	• Teacher discusses words regularly and posts them around the room.	• Teacher thinks out loud about confusing points or misunderstandings about the text.	
	• Teacher discusses new or confusing vocabulary words and encourages inferences.	• Teacher discusses unknown or confusing vocabulary words and encourages inferences.	
	• Teacher stops at points in the book to check students' listening comprehension, focusing on *who, what, why, when,* and *where* questions.		
	• Teacher encourages talk and responds to what students are saying, rather than correcting how they are saying it.		

Shared Reading • Look-For Bank

LOOK-FOR CATEGORIES	KINDERGARTEN	GRADE 1	GRADE 2
Environment	• Complex and engaging text is used for shared reading (i.e., texts that have multiple levels of meaning appropriate for the grade level, and contain complex and/or multiple themes and language that is not too simple). There is a balance between fiction and nonfiction. • The classroom library is large and contains an extensive range of topics, text types, and genres. • The classroom is filled with books and other texts on a variety of topics and in a variety of genres, and reflect students' races, cultures, and identities.		
Print Concepts	• Understand parts of the book. • Practice directionality: left to right, top to bottom, page by page. • Separate written words with spaces. • Recognize simple punctuation. • Recognize upper- and lowercase letters.	• Understand basic features and organization of print (e.g., basic features of a sentence).	
Phonics	• Count words in sentences. • Isolate and pronounce initial phonemes in CVC words (e.g., *cat*). • Isolate and pronounce medial phonemes in CVC words. • Isolate and pronounce final phonemes in CVC words. • Decode to segment and blend simple words.	• Distinguish between similarly spelled words by identifying different sounds of letters. • Read common irregular words. Segment sounds to write words.	
		• Decode (segment and blend) two-syllable words by breaking them into syllables. • Recognize sound-spelling correspondences with common consonant digraphs (e.g., *th*) and blends (e.g., *st*). • Decode long-vowel sounds in regularly spelled one-syllable words (e.g., final *-e* and common vowel teams).	• Distinguish long and short vowels in regular one-syllable words (CVC and CVCe words). • Know sound-spelling correspondences for common vowel teams. • Decode (segment and blend) two-syllable words with long vowels. • Decode words with prefixes and suffixes. • Identify words with inconsistent but common sound-spelling correspondences. • Self-monitor and apply word-reading skills to self-correct.
Fluency	• Are exposed to fluent oral reading (e.g., phrasing and expression).		• Read and write common high-frequency words and sight words.
	• Recognize common high-frequency words and sight words.	• Read common high-frequency words and sight words.	• Read appropriate texts with purpose and meaning. • Read appropriate texts, including stories, poetry, and nonfiction, with accuracy and adequate phrasing and expression to support comprehension. • Reread and use context to confirm or self-correct word recognition and comprehension.

Shared Reading • Look-For Bank

LOOK-FOR CATEGORIES	KINDERGARTEN	GRADE 1	GRADE 2
Comprehension	• Teacher points out and clarifies new vocabulary words. • Make predictions about what will happen in a story, based on text details and prior knowledge.		
	• Recognize genre and genre features. • Ask and answer questions about the text. • Describe the illustrations and the meaning illustrations provide to the text. • Identify the main topic and key details in nonfiction texts.		
		• Retell the story, including key details, and discuss the central message or theme of the story. • Identify who is telling the story. • Identify the author's point of view and, for nonfiction, the author's purpose for writing the text. • Describe connections between individuals, ideas, events, and information in a text.	
			• Use information from words and pictures to describe characters, setting, and plot. • Use information from text features (e.g., diagrams, photographs) to understand main points. • Use common affixes and roots to determine word meanings. • Think through earlier predictions and why they were or were not correct, referring to the text for details. • Identify the author's purpose for writing a nonfiction text. • Describe how text evidence supports the author's point(s).
Engagement	• Engage in collaborative conversations about text, story, and nonfiction topics. • Discuss big ideas related to the text read collaboratively. • Are central to the discussion, and do the majority of thinking and talking about texts. • Listen to others and take turns talking. • Speak audibly and independently. • Teacher discusses confusing points or misunderstandings about the text. • Teacher discusses new or confusing vocabulary words and encourages inferences.		
		• Listen to and discuss a book or chapter that is longer and more difficult than a book or chapter that can be read independently or with assistance.	
			• Add to one another's comments.

Shared Reading • Look-For Bank

LOOK-FOR CATEGORIES	GRADE 3	GRADE 4	GRADE 5
Environment	• Complex and engaging text is used for shared reading (i.e., texts that have multiple levels of meaning appropriate for the grade level, and contain complex and/or multiple themes and language that is not too simple). There is a balance between fiction and nonfiction. • The classroom library is large and contains an extensive range of topics, text types, and genres. • The classroom is filled with books and other texts on a variety of topics and in a variety of genres, and reflect students' races, cultures, and identities.		
Phonics	• Identify and know the meaning of common prefixes and derivational suffixes (i.e., suffixes that make [derive] new words). • Decode words with common Latin suffixes. • Decode (segment and blend) multisyllabic words. • Read grade-level appropriate irregularly spelled words. • Segment words into syllables to spell them. • Self-monitor and apply word-reading skills to self-correct.	• Use grade-level phonics and word-analysis skills to decode words. • Use knowledge of all letter-sound correspondences to decode unfamiliar multisyllabic words in context and out of context. • Use knowledge of syllabication patterns to decode unfamiliar multisyllabic words in context and out of context. • Use knowledge of prefixes, suffixes, and root words to decode unfamiliar multisyllabic words in context and out of context.	
Fluency	• Read appropriate texts with purpose and meaning. • Read appropriate texts, including stories, poetry, and nonfiction, with accuracy and adequate phrasing and expression to support comprehension. • Reread and use context to confirm or self-correct word recognition and comprehension.		
Comprehension	• Teacher points out and clarifies new vocabulary words. • Make predictions about what will happen in a story based on text details and prior knowledge. • Think through earlier predictions and why they were or were not correct, referring to the text for details. • Identify the author's purpose for writing a nonfiction text. • Describe how text evidence supports the author's point(s). • Determine the main idea of a text and explain how key details support it. • Distinguish their own point of view from the narrator and characters' points of view.		
	• Describe logical connections between sentences and paragraphs in a text. • Compare and contrast the most important points and key details in two texts on the same topic. • Use information from words and pictures to describe characters, setting, and plot. • Use information from text features (e.g., diagrams, photographs) to understand main points. • Use common affixes and roots to determine word meanings.	• Use Greek and Latin Roots and affixes to determine word meanings. • Summarize the text using details and information drawn from it. • Determine themes in a story, drama, or poem from details it contains. • Draw inferences from a text, using details from the text to support them. • Compare and contrast themes and topics (e.g., good vs. evil) across more than two texts. • Explain events, procedures, ideas, or concepts in a historical, scientific, or technical text, including what happened and why, based on text details. • Interpret information presented visually, orally, or quantitatively (e.g., charts, graphs, timelines, diagrams, animations) and explain how the information contributes to an understanding of the text.	

Shared Reading • Look-For Bank

LOOK-FOR CATEGORIES	GRADE 3	GRADE 4	GRADE 5
Comprehension (cont.)		• Refer to details and examples in a text when explaining what it says explicitly. • Describe in depth a character (traits, thoughts, actions), setting, or event in a story or drama, drawing on specific details. • Compare and contrast the point of view from which different stories are narrated, including first and third person. • Explain structural differences between poetry, drama, and prose. • Explain how an author uses reasons and evidence to support points. • Describe the structure (e.g., chronology, comparison, cause/effect, problem/solution) of events, ideas, concepts, or information in a text or part of a text.	• Refer to details, examples, and quotes when explaining what the text says explicitly. • Describe how characters in a story respond to challenges. • Describe how the narrator of a poem reflects on a topic. • Compare and contrast characters (traits, thoughts, actions) in a story, drawing on specific details it contains. • Describe how the narrator's point of view influences descriptions of events. • Determine two or more main ideas in the text and explain how key details support them. • Explain the relationships or interactions between two or more individuals, events, ideas, or concepts in a historical, scientific, or technical text, based on specific information it contains. • Integrate information from two texts on the same topic to write or speak about the topic knowledgeably. • Compare and contrast texts in the same genre or with similar themes or topics. • Point out and clarify new vocabulary words and phrases, including domain-specific words, and literary techniques, such as metaphors and similes. • Compare and contrast the overall structure (e.g., chronology, comparison, cause/effect, problem/solution) of events, ideas, concepts, or information in two or more texts. • Analyze multiple accounts of the same event or topic, noting important similarities and differences in the point of view they represent.

Shared Reading • Look-For Bank

LOOK-FOR CATEGORIES	GRADE 3	GRADE 4	GRADE 5
Engagement	• Engage in collaborative conversations about text, story, and nonfiction topics. • Discuss big ideas related to the text read collaboratively. • Are central to the discussion, and do the majority of thinking and talking about texts. • Listen to others and take turns talking. • Speak audibly and independently. • Teacher discusses confusing points or misunderstandings about the text. • Teacher discusses new or confusing vocabulary words and encourages inferences. • Listen to and discuss a book or chapter that is longer and more difficult than a book or chapter that can be read independently or with assistance. • Add to one another's comments.		

Shared Reading · Look-For Bank

LOOK-FOR CATEGORIES	GRADE 6	GRADE 7	GRADE 8
Environment	• Complex and engaging text is used for shared reading (i.e., texts that have multiple levels of meaning appropriate for the grade level, and contain complex and/or multiple themes and language that is not too simple). There is a balance between fiction and nonfiction. • The classroom library is large and contains an extensive range of topics, text types, and genres. • The classroom is filled with books and other texts on a variety of topics and in a variety of genres, and reflect students' races, cultures, and identities.		
Fluency	• Read appropriate texts with purpose and meaning. • Read appropriate texts, including stories, poetry, and nonfiction, with accuracy and adequate phrasing and expression to support comprehension. • Reread and use context to confirm or self-correct word recognition and comprehension.		
		• Identify and know the meaning of common prefixes and derivational suffixes (e.g., suffixes that make new words).	
Comprehension	• Summarize texts objectively, without personal opinions. • Analyze how a sentence, chapter, scene, or stanza helps to develop theme, character, setting, or plot. • Explain how the author develops the narrator, character, or subject's point of view.		
	• Think through earlier predictions and why they were or were not correct, referring to the text for details. • Identify the author's purpose for writing a nonfiction text. • Describe how text evidence supports the author's point(s). • Determine the main idea of a text and explain how key details support it. • Distinguish their own point of view from the narrator and characters' points of view. • Draw inferences from a text, using details from the text to support them. • Compare and contrast themes and topics (e.g., good vs. evil) across more than two texts. • Explain events, procedures, ideas, or concepts in a historical, scientific, or technical text, including what happened and why, based on text details. • Interpret information presented visually, orally, or quantitatively (e.g., charts, graphs, timelines, diagrams, animations) and explain how the information contributes to an understanding of the text.	• Cite several pieces of textual evidence to support analysis of what the text says explicitly. • Draw inferences from the text, using details and quotes from text to support inferences. • Compare and contrast the fictional portrayal of a time, place, or character and a historical account of the same period as a means of understanding how authors of fiction use or alter history. • Analyze how modern fiction draws on traditional themes. • Think through earlier predictions and why they did or did not come true, referring to the text explicitly for details. • Determine the meaning of words and phrases as they are used in a text, including analogies, allusions, and figurative, connotative, and technical meanings. • Analyze the impact of word choice on meaning and tone. • Analyze how two or more authors writing about the same topic shape their presentations of key information by emphasizing different interpretation of texts or presenting different interpretations of facts.	
		• Determine a theme or central ideas in a text and analyze development of the theme or central idea throughout the text. • Analyze how particular elements of a story interact. • Determine the central idea of a nonfiction text and analyze its development through the text.	• Determine multiple themes or central ideas in a text and analyze development of the theme or central idea throughout the text, including the relationship of the theme to characters, setting and plot. • Analyze how particular lines of dialogue or incidents in a story propel the action, reveal aspects of character, or lead to a decision or turning point in the story.

Shared Reading • Look-For Bank

Grades 6–8

LOOK-FOR CATEGORIES	GRADE 6	GRADE 7	GRADE 8
Comprehension (cont.)	• Compare and contrast the overall structure (e.g., chronology, comparison, cause/effect, problem/solution) of events, ideas, concepts, or information in two or more texts. • Analyze multiple accounts of the same event or topic, noting important similarities and differences in the point of view they represent. • Analyze what a text says, citing evidence from it. • Determine a text's theme or central idea and explain how it is conveyed through details. • Describe how a story or drama's plot unfolds, as well as how the characters respond or change. • Trace and evaluate a text for arguments and claims. • Compare and contrast one author's presentation of events with another's. • Analyze how a sentence, paragraph, chapter, or section fits into a text's overall structure and contributes to the development of the ideas. • Determine the meaning of a text's words and phrases, including figurative, connotative, and technical meanings.	• Trace and evaluate the argument and specific claims in a text, assessing whether the reasoning is sound and evidence is relevant and/or sufficient to support the claims. • Compare and contrast the overall structure (e.g., chronology, comparison, cause/effect, problem/solution) of events, ideas, concepts, or information in two or more texts and compare them to multimedia representations of the text. • Analyze the structure an author uses to organize a text, including how the major sections contribute to the whole and to the development of the idea.	• Compare and contrast the structure of two or more texts, describing how the structure relates to meaning and style. • Analyze how differences in points of view of the characters in the story create effects, such as suspense or humor. • Analyze in detail the structure of a specific paragraph, considering how the sentences in the paragraph define and refine a key concept. • Determine the author's point of view or purpose for writing a text and analyze how the author acknowledges and responds to conflicting evidence or viewpoints. • Delineate and evaluate the argument and specific claims in a text, assessing whether the reasoning is sound and recognizing irrelevant evidence.
Engagement	\multicolumn{3}{l}{• Are central to the discussion and do the majority of thinking and talking about texts. • Listen to others and take turns talking. • Speak audibly and independently. • Listen to and discuss a book or chapter that is longer and more difficult than a book or chapter that can be read independently or with assistance. • Teacher discusses new or confusing vocabulary words and encourages inferences. • Add to one another's comments.}		
	• Engage in collaborative conversations about text, story, and nonfiction topics. • Discuss big ideas related to the text read collaboratively. • Teacher discusses confusing points or misunderstandings about the text.	• Discuss confusing points or misunderstandings about one another's point of view or presentation of big ideas. • Teacher facilitates collaborative conversation about text, story, and nonfiction topics based on a big idea that arises from the text.	

114

TM ® & © Scholastic Inc. All rights reserved. *Literacy Walks* copyright © 2021 by Nancy Akhavan. Published by Scholastic Inc.

Small-Group and Independent Reading Look-For Bank

LOOK-FOR CATEGORIES	KINDERGARTEN	GRADE 1	GRADE 2
Environment	• Appropriate text is used, including leveled text, decodable text, and language-controlled text. There is a balance between fiction and nonfiction. • Each student has a personalized, individual book bag or box for independent reading. • The classroom library is large and contains an extensive range of topics, text types, and genres. • The classroom is filled with books and other texts on a variety of topics and in a variety of genres, and reflect students' races, cultures, and identities.		
Print Concepts	• Understand parts of the book. • Practice directionality: left to right, top to bottom, page by page. • Recognize simple punctuation. • Recognize upper- and lowercase letters. • Recognize spaces between words. • Match spoken words to print, with specific sequences of letters. • Ask and answer questions about the illustrations and how they enhance the text's meaning. • Reread the text and study illustrations to guide understanding.	• Understand basic features and organization of print (e.g., basic features of a sentence).	
Phonics	• Segment sounds to write words. • Distinguish between similarly spelled words by identifying different sounds of letters.		
	• Identify letter sounds. • Use initial letters to figure out new words. • Segment sounds to read new words. • Blend sounds to read new words. • Use meaning, known words, and initial letters to self-monitor while reading. • Segment sounds to write new words.	• Read common irregular words. • Self-monitor and apply word-reading skills to self-correct.	
		• Decode (segment and blend) single-syllable words. • Decode (segment and blend) two-syllable words by breaking them into syllables. • Recognize sound-spelling correspondences with common consonant digraphs (e.g., *th*) and blends (e.g., *st*). • Blend onsets and rimes. • Decode long-vowel sounds in regularly spelled one-syllable words (e.g., final -*e* and common vowel teams). • Know that every syllable must have a vowel sound. • Read words with inflectional endings (e.g., -*s*, -*er*, -*ing*).	• Distinguish long and short vowels in regular one-syllable words (CVC and CVCe words). • Know sound-spelling correspondences for common vowel teams. • Decode (segment and blend) two-syllable words with long vowels. • Point out words with prefixes and suffixes. • Identify words with inconsistent but common word sound-spelling correspondences.

Small-Group and Independent Reading Look-For Bank

LOOK-FOR CATEGORIES	KINDERGARTEN	GRADE 1	GRADE 2
Fluency	• Read and write common high-frequency words and sight words.		
		• Read appropriate texts with accuracy and adequate phrasing to support comprehension.	• Read appropriate texts with purpose and meaning. • Read appropriate texts, including stories, poetry, and nonfiction, with accuracy and adequate fluency and phrasing to support comprehension. • Reread and use context to confirm or self-correct word recognition and comprehension.
Comprehension	• Teacher points out and clarifies new vocabulary words. • Make predictions about what will happen next in the story based on details and prior knowledge of the text.		
	• Recognize major differences between genres and genre features. • Ask and answer questions about the text.		
	• Discuss a story with prompting. • Ask and answer questions about the text. • Describe beginning, middle, and end details in nonfiction texts. • Attend to new vocabulary words. • Recognize and discuss beginnings, middle details, and endings in fiction texts. • Discuss characters and character experiences, thoughts, and feelings. • Discuss how details support important points in nonfiction text; identify the author's purpose for writing the text.	• Retell the story including key details and discuss the central message or theme of the story. • Identify who is telling the story. • Identify author point of view and, for nonfiction, the author's purpose for writing the text. • Describe connections between individuals, ideas, events, and information in a text. • Think through earlier predictions and why they did or did not come true, referring to the text explicitly for details.	
		• Describe the illustrations and the meaning illustrations provide to the text. • Use illustrations and details to describe characters, setting, and events. • Describe characters, settings, and major events in the story, noting details. • Identify the main topic and key details in nonfiction texts. • Describe how details support important points in nonfiction text.	• Use common affixes and roots to determine word meanings. • Ask and answer *who, what, why, when,* and *where* questions to demonstrate understanding of the text. • Use details to describe how characters respond to major events in the story. • Describe plot, noting how details in the beginning and middle lead to the ending. • Acknowledge differences in the points of view of characters, including speaking in a different voice when reading aloud.

Small-Group and Independent Reading Look-For Bank

LOOK-FOR CATEGORIES	KINDERGARTEN	GRADE 1	GRADE 2
Comprehension (cont.)			• Use information from words and pictures to describe characters, setting, and plot. • Describe how text evidence supports the author's point(s). • Identify main topic and key details of multi-paragraph nonfiction texts, as well as the topic of individual paragraphs. • Compare and contrast stories and texts on the same subject or topic. • Describe connections between events, ideas, or concepts in nonfiction texts, including historical, scientific, and procedural texts. • Use information from text features (e.g., diagrams, photographs, graphs) to understand main points.
Engagement	• Engage in collaborative conversations about text, story, and nonfiction topics. • Speak audibly and independently.		
		• Are central to the discussion, and do the majority of thinking and talking about texts. • Express self in complete sentences. • Teacher discusses confusing points or misunderstandings about the text. • Teacher discusses new or confusing vocabulary words and encourages inferences.	

Small-Group and Independent Reading Look-For Bank

LOOK-FOR CATEGORIES	GRADE 3	GRADE 4	GRADE 5
Environment	• Appropriate text is used, including leveled text, decodable text, and language-controlled text. There is a balance between fiction and nonfiction. • Each student has a personalized, individual book bag or box for independent reading. • The classroom library is large and contains an extensive range of topics, text types, and genres. • The classroom is filled with books and other texts on a variety of topics and in a variety of genres, and reflect students' races, cultures, and identities.		
Phonics	• Segment sounds to write words. • Distinguish between similarly spelled words by identifying different sounds of letters. • Identify and know the meaning of common prefixes and derivational suffixes (i.e., suffixes that make [derive] new words). • Decode words with common Latin suffixes. • Decode (segment and blend) multisyllabic words. • Segment words into syllables to spell them. • Read common irregular words. • Self-monitor and apply word-reading skills to self-correct.	• Use grade-level phonics and word-analysis skills to decode words. • Use knowledge of all letter-sound correspondences to decode unfamiliar multisyllabic words. • Use knowledge of syllabication patterns to decode unfamiliar multisyllabic words in context and out of context. • Use knowledge of prefixes, suffixes, and root words to decode unfamiliar multisyllabic words in context and out of context.	
Fluency	• Read appropriate texts with purpose and meaning. • Read appropriate texts, including stories, poetry, and nonfiction, with accuracy and adequate fluency and phrasing to support comprehension. • Reread and use context to confirm or self-correct word recognition and comprehension.		
	• Read and write common high-frequency words and sight words.		
Comprehension	• Teacher points out and clarifies new vocabulary words. • Make predictions about what will happen next in the story based on details and prior knowledge of the text. • Think through earlier predictions and why they did or did not come true, referring to the text explicitly for details. • Identify the author's point of view. • Identify the author's purpose for writing the text. • Describe how text evidence supports the author's points(s). • Determine the main idea of a text and explain how key details support it. • Distinguish their own point of view apart from the narrator's and characters' points of view. • Use common affixes and roots to determine word meanings.		

Small-Group and Independent Reading Look-For Bank

LOOK-FOR CATEGORIES	GRADE 3	GRADE 4	GRADE 5
Comprehension (cont.)	• Ask questions about text and explicitly refer to the text to answer them. • Describe stories; determine central messages and identify them with details from the text. • Use details to describe a character's thoughts, feelings, and traits, and how the character's actions contribute to the sequence of events. • Describe books, stories, poems, and other texts, and discuss how each chapter, scene, or stanza builds on one another. • Compare and contrast themes, settings, and plots of books in a series. • Distinguish their own point of view from the narrator's and characters' points of view. • Describe relationships between ideas, events, concepts, and information in a text, using cause and effect, time and sequence, etc. • Describe connections between sentences and paragraphs in a text. • Compare and contrast the most important points and key details in two texts on the same topic. • Use information from words and pictures to describe characters, setting, and plot. • Use information from text features (e.g., diagrams, photographs, graphs) to understand main points.	• Refer to details and examples in a text when explaining what it says explicitly. • Draw inferences from a text, using details from the text to support them. • Summarize the text using details and information drawn from it. • Describe in depth a character (traits, thoughts, actions), setting, or event in a story or drama, drawing on specific details. • Compare and contrast the point of view from which different stories are narrated, including first and third person. • Compare and contrast themes and topics (e.g., good vs. evil) across more than two texts. • Explain how an author uses reasons and evidence to support points. • Integrate information from two texts on the same topic to write or speak about the topic knowledgeably. • Explain events, procedures, ideas, or concepts in a historical, scientific, or technical text, including what happened and why, based on text details. • Interpret information presented visually, orally, or quantitatively (e.g., charts, graphs, timelines, diagrams, animations) and explain how the information contributes to an understanding of the text. • Describe the structure (e.g., chronology, comparison, cause/effect, problem/solution) of events, ideas, concepts, or information in a text or part of a text. • Compare and contrast a firsthand and secondhand account of an event; describe the differences in focus and the information provided; examine primary documents. • Use Greek and Latin roots and affixes to determine word meanings. • Determine themes in a story, drama, or poem from details it contains.	
Engagement	• Engage in collaborative conversations about text, story, and nonfiction topics. • Speak audibly and independently. • Are central to the discussion, and do the majority of thinking and talking about texts. • Express self in complete sentences. • Teacher discusses confusing points or misunderstandings about the text. • Teacher discusses new or confusing vocabulary and encourages inferences.		

Small-Group and Independent Reading Look-For Bank

LOOK-FOR CATEGORIES	GRADE 6	GRADE 7	GRADE 8
Environment	• The classroom library is large and contains an extensive range of topics, text types, and genres. • The classroom is filled with books and other texts on a variety of topics and in a variety of genres, and reflect students' races, cultures, and identities.		
	• Appropriate text is used, including leveled text, decodable text, and language-controlled text. There is a balance between fiction and nonfiction. • Each student has a personalized, individual book bag or box for independent reading.	• Rich, complex texts are available in a variety of genres, topics, and themes. There is a balance of fiction and nonfiction. • Students have access to books which they can read independently and for grade-level instruction.	
Phonics	• Use grade-level phonics and word-analysis skills to decode words. • Use knowledge of prefixes, suffixes, and root words to decode unfamiliar multisyllabic words in context and out of context. • Use syllabication patterns as a clue to spell words conventionally. • Spell common irregular words correctly. • Build words using Latin and Greek roots with prefixes and suffixes.		
	• Use knowledge of syllabication patterns to decode unfamiliar multisyllabic words in context and out of context.		• Decode unfamiliar multisyllabic words in context and out of context.
	• Use knowledge of all letter-sound correspondences to decode unfamiliar multisyllabic words. • Use knowledge of prefixes, suffixes, and root words to decode unfamiliar multisyllabic words in context and out of context. • Use syllabication patterns as a clue to spell words conventionally.	• Use knowledge of all letter-sound correspondences to decode unfamiliar multisyllabic words in context and out of context.	
Fluency	• Read appropriate texts with purpose and meaning. • Reread and use context to confirm or self-correct word recognition and understanding. • Read appropriate texts, including stories, poetry, and nonfiction, with accuracy and adequate fluency and phrasing to support comprehension.		
		• Identify and know the meaning of common prefixes and derivational suffixes (i.e., suffixes that make new words).	

Small-Group and Independent Reading Look-For Bank

LOOK-FOR CATEGORIES	GRADE 6	GRADE 7	GRADE 8
Comprehension	• Draw inferences from a text, using details from the text to support them.		
	• Teacher points out and clarifies new vocabulary words. • Make predictions about what will happen next in the story, based on details and prior knowledge of the text. • Think through earlier predictions and why they did or did not come true, referring to the text explicitly for details. • Identify author's point of view and, for nonfiction, the author's purpose for writing the text.	• Cite several pieces of textual evidence to support analysis of what the text says explicitly. • Compare and contrast the fictional portrayal of a time, place, or character and a historical account of the same period as a means of understanding how authors of fiction use or alter history. • Analyze how modern fiction draws on traditional themes. • Think through earlier predictions and why they did or did not come true, referring to the text explicitly for details. • Determine the meaning of words and phrases as they are used in a text, including analogies, allusions, and figurative, connotative, and technical meanings. • Analyze the impact of word choice on meaning and tone. • Summarize texts objectively without personal opinions.	
	• Describe how text evidence supports the author's point(s). • Determine main idea of a text and explain how key details support it. • Distinguish their own point of view apart from the narrator and character's point of view. • Refer to details and examples in a text when explaining what it says explicitly. Summarize the text using details and information drawn from it. • Describe in depth a character (traits, thoughts, actions), setting, or event in a story or drama, drawing on specific details. • Compare and contrast the point of view from which different stories are narrated, including first and third person. • Compare and contrast themes and topics (e.g., good vs. evil) across more than two texts. • Explain how an author uses reasons and evidence to support points. • Integrate information from two texts on the same topic to write or speak about the topic knowledgeably.	• Determine a theme or central ideas in a text and analyze development of the theme or central idea throughout the text. • Analyze how particular elements of a story interact. • Explain how an author develops and contrasts the point of view of the narrator or speaker in a text. • Analyze how a particular sentence, chapter, scene, or stanza contributes to the development of the theme, setting, or plot. • Trace and evaluate the argument and specific claims in a text, assessing whether the reasoning is sound and evidence is relevant and/or sufficient to support the claims. • Analyze how two or more authors writing about the same topic shape their presentations of key information by emphasizing different interpretation of texts or presenting different interpretations of facts.	• Determine multiple themes or central ideas in a text and analyze development of the theme or central idea throughout the text, including the relationship of the theme to characters, setting, and plot. • Analyze how particular lines of dialogue or incidents in a story propel the action, reveal aspects of character, or lead to a decision or turning point in the story. • Compare and contrast structure of two or more texts, describing how the structure relates to meaning and style. • Analyze how differences in points of view of the characters in the story create effects such as suspense or humor. • Determine the central idea of a nonfiction text and analyze its development through the text. • Analyze in detail the structure of a specific paragraph, considering how the sentences in the paragraph define and refine a key concept.

Literacy Walks copyright © 2021 by Nancy Akhavan. Published by Scholastic Inc.

Small-Group and Independent Reading Look-For Bank

LOOK-FOR CATEGORIES	GRADE 6	GRADE 7	GRADE 8
Comprehension (cont.)	• Explain events, procedures, ideas, or concepts in a historical, scientific, or technical text, including what happened and why, based on text details. • Interpret information presented visually, orally, or quantitatively (e.g., charts, graphs, timelines, diagrams, animations) and explain how the information contributes to an understanding of the text. • Describe the structure (e.g., chronology, comparison, cause/effect, problem/ solution) of events, ideas, concepts, or information in a text or part of a text. • Compare and contrast a firsthand and secondhand account of an event; describe the differences in focus and the information provided; examine primary documents. • Use Greek and Latin roots and affixes to determine word meanings.	• Compare and contrast the overall structure (e.g., chronology, comparison, cause/effect, problem/ solution) of events, ideas, concepts, or information in two or more texts and compare them to multimedia representations of the text. • Analyze the structure an author uses to organize a text, including how the major sections contribute to the whole and to the development of the idea.	• Determine an author's point of view or purpose for writing a text and analyze how the author acknowledges and responds to conflicting evidence or viewpoints. • Delineate and evaluate the argument and specific claims in a text, assessing whether the reasoning is sound and recognizing irrelevant evidence.
Engagement	• Are central to the discussion, and do the majority of thinking and talking about texts. • Speak audibly and independently.		
	• Engage in collaborative conversations about text, story, and nonfiction topics. • Express self in complete sentences. • Teacher discusses confusing points or misunderstandings about the text. • Teacher discusses new or confusing vocabulary and encourages inferences.	• Listen to others and take turns talking. • Add onto one another's comments. • Discuss confusing points or misunderstandings about one another's point of view or presentation of big ideas. • Teacher facilitates collaborative conversation about text, story, and nonfiction topics based on a big idea that arises from the text.	

Writing • Look-For Bank

LOOK-FOR CATEGORIES	KINDERGARTEN	GRADE 1	GRADE 2
Environment	• Complex and engaging books are used as mentor texts to demonstrate the writing craft. There is a balance between fiction and nonfiction. • Books are displayed around the room, and students have access to them while writing. • The classroom is filled with books and other texts on a variety of topics and in a variety of genres, and reflect students' races, cultures, and identities.		
Composition	• Ask for feedback and respond to writing. • Write in a variety of genres, the including personal narrative, fiction, explanatory, description, and opinion. • Work with peer or adult to strengthen the writing by responding to questions, considering suggestions, or asking for clarification. • Participate in individual, shared, and group writing, inquiry, and/or research projects. • Participate in group composition (e.g., add ideas, expand sentences) during shared writing.		
		• Write a response to a text, author, or theme. • Use a variety of digital tools to produce and publish writing, collaborating with peers.	
	• Draw, write, and/or dictate to compose original writing. • Generate topics and content for writing. • With narrative writing, include a single event or several events loosely linked together. • With explanatory, descriptive, or informative writing, stay on topic and provide some detail. • With opinion writing, state an opinion.		• Compose original writing, generating topics and content. • With narrative writing, include details to describe an event and actions, thoughts, and feelings of characters. • Organize narrative writing logically and develop it well; include a logical conclusion. • With opinion writing, state an opinion and provide clear reasons for it; include a concluding statement or section. • With opinion writing, use linking words to connect reasons for the opinion. • Use temporal words to add meaning. • Recall information from experience or gather information from print and digital sources in anticipation of the reader's questions. • Brainstorm, draft, revise, edit, and polish writing. • With explanatory, descriptive, or informative writing, introduce a topic and use details and definitions to develop it; include a concluding statement or section.

Writing • Look-For Bank

LOOK-FOR CATEGORIES	KINDERGARTEN	GRADE 1	GRADE 2
Mechanics	• Write upper- and lowercase letters, begin sentences with uppercase letters, and start proper names with uppercase letters. • Write from left to right, top to bottom. • Attempt simple end punctuation. • Add spaces between words and sentences.	• Write upper- and lowercase letters, begin sentences with uppercase letters, write proper names with uppercase letters. • Use common adjectives, prepositions, and conjunctions. • Include spaces between words and sentences. • Use conventional spelling.	
		• Use simple punctuation. • Produce and expand simple and compound sentences with adult support.	• Use punctuation, including apostrophes and commas. • Produce, expand, and rearrange complete simple and compound sentences. • Express self in simple and compound sentences, and other sentence types.
Phonics	• Segment sounds to write new words phonetically. • Write common high-frequency words and sight words.		
	• Encode by listening to words and writing initial sounds. • Encode by listening to words and writing medial sounds. • Encode by listening to words and writing final sounds.	• Encode by listening to new words and writing letters to represent the sounds in those words.	

Writing • Look-For Bank

LOOK-FOR CATEGORIES	GRADE 3	GRADE 4	GRADE 5
Environment	• Complex and engaging books are used as mentor texts to demonstrate writing craft. There is a balance between fiction and nonfiction. • Books are displayed around the room, and students have access to them while writing. • The classroom is filled with books and other texts on a variety of topics and in a variety of genres, and reflect students' races, cultures, and identities.		
Composition	• Compose original writing, generating topics and content. • Write in a variety of genres, including personal narrative, fiction, explanatory, description, and opinion. • Work with peer or adult to strengthen the writing by responding to questions, considering suggestions, or asking for clarification. • Participate in individual, shared, and group writing, inquiry, and/or research projects. • Participate in group composition (e.g., add ideas, expand sentences) during shared writing. • Write a response to a text, author, or theme. • Use a variety of digital tools to produce and publish writing, collaborating with peers. • Brainstorm, draft, revise, edit, and polish writing. • With explanatory, descriptive, or informative writing, introduce a topic and use details and definitions to develop it; include a concluding statement or section.		
	• Ask for feedback and respond to writing. • With narrative writing, include details to describe an event and actions, thoughts, and feelings of characters. • Organize narrative writing logically and develop it well; include a logical conclusion. • With opinion writing, state an opinion and provide clear reasons for it; include a concluding statement or section. • With opinion writing, use linking words to connect reasons for the opinion. • Use temporal words to add meaning.	• With explanatory, descriptive, or informative writing, introduce a topic clearly and group relevant information in paragraphs and sections. • Include formatting (e.g., headings), illustrations, and multimedia when useful to aiding comprehension. • Ask for feedback and respond to writing, referring explicitly to areas of the piece that need to be clarified or otherwise improved. • With narrative writing, establish a situation real or imagined and introduce a narrator and/or characters; sequence unfolds naturally. • Use dialogue and description to develop the situation and convey reactions of characters. • Organize and develop the piece well; include a conclusion that brings closure to the experience, event, or plot. • Develop topics with facts, definitions, quotes, and information from reliable sources. • Connect ideas and information using linking words and phrases. • Use precise domain-specific vocabulary and a variety of transition words and phrases. • Use relevant information from experiences or gather relevant information from print and digital sources; take and categorize notes and list sources. • Draw evidence from literary or informational texts to support analysis, reflection, and research. • Recall information from experience or gather information from print and digital sources in anticipation of the reader's questions. • Link ideas and information together using words and phrases.	

Writing • Look-For Bank

LOOK-FOR CATEGORIES	GRADE 3	GRADE 4	GRADE 5
Composition (cont.)		• With narrative writing, use concrete language and sensory details. • With opinion writing, offer a point of view and provide clear reasons and evidence (i.e., facts and details) for the opinion; organize writing by grouping related ideas to support point of view. • Provide a concluding statement for an opinion.	• With narrative writing, use concrete language, sensory details, and precise language to convey experiences and events. • With opinion writing, offer a point of view and provide clear reasons and evidence (i.e., facts and details) for the opinion; organize writing by grouping related ideas to support point of view and including a concluding section or statement. • Organize explanatory, descriptive, or informative writing logically and include headings, illustrations, and multimedia. • Organize opinion writing logically and include reasons to support opinions, supported by facts and details.
Mechanics	• Use conventional spelling. • Express self in simple and compound sentences and other sentence types.		
	• Use punctuation, including apostrophes and commas. • Produce, expand, and rearrange complete simple and compound sentences. • Write upper- and lowercase letters, begin sentences with uppercase letters, write proper names with uppercase letters. • Use common adjectives, prepositions, and conjunctions. • Include spaces between words and sentences.	• Use correct punctuation, including commas and quotation marks.	
		• Use punctuation for effect.	• Use punctuation for effect and to separate items in a series. • Use commas to separate introductory phrases and other elements from rest of the sentence. • Use commas to set apart specific words in a sentence. • Use conventional spelling and consult resources as necessary. • Use underlining, quotation marks, or italics to indicate titles of works. • Use correlative conjunctions. • Recognize fragments and run-on sentences.

Writing • Look-For Bank

LOOK-FOR CATEGORIES	GRADE 6	GRADE 7	GRADE 8
Environment	• Complex and engaging books are used as mentor texts to demonstrate writing craft. There is a balance between fiction and nonfiction. • Books are displayed around the room, and students have access to them while writing. • The classroom is filled with books and other texts on a variety of topics and in a variety of genres, and reflect students' races, cultures, and identities.		
Composition	• Compose original writing, generating topics and content. • Ask for feedback and respond to writing, referring explicitly to areas of the piece that need to be clarified or otherwise improved. • Use dialogue and description to develop the situation and convey reactions of characters. • With explanatory, descriptive, or informative writing, introduce a topic or thesis statement and group relevant information in paragraphs and sections to support the statement. • Use precise domain-specific vocabulary and a variety of transition words and phrases. • Draw evidence from literary or informational texts to support analysis, reflection, and research. • Participate in group composition (e.g., add ideas, expand sentences) during shared writing. • Use relevant information from experiences or gather relevant information from print and digital sources; take and categorize notes and list sources.		
	• Write in a variety of genres, including personal narrative, fiction, explanatory, description, and opinion. • Work with peer or adult to strengthen the writing by responding to questions, considering suggestions, or asking for clarification. • Participate in individual, shared, and group writing, inquiry, and/or research projects. • Write a response to a text, author, or theme. • Use a variety of digital tools to produce and publish writing, collaborating with peers. • With narrative writing, use effective techniques, relevant descriptive details, and a well-structured sequence of events. • With explanatory, descriptive, or informative writing, introduce and examine a topic. • Convey ideas, concepts, and information through the selection and organization of relevant content. • Carefully choose relevant content to include in the writing.	• Write in a variety of genres, including personal narrative, fictional narrative, explanatory, description, and argument. • Choose writing that expresses ideas precisely and concisely, recognizing and eliminating wordiness and redundancy. • With narrative writing, establish a situation and introduce a narrator and/or characters; make sure the sequence unfolds naturally; use a variety of transition words, phrases, and clauses; use precise words and phrases. • With narrative writing, use effective techniques, relevant descriptive details, and a well-structured sequence of events, including a conclusion that follows from the text and reflects on the narrated experiences. • Explanatory, description, or informative writing introduces a topic or thesis statement and groups. Group relevant information together in paragraphs and sections to support the thesis statement, previewing what is to follow after the thesis statement. • Use appropriate transitions to create cohesion and clarify the relationships among ideas and concepts. • Develop topics with examples, facts, definitions, quotes, and information that references what they have read or researched. • Argument writing states a claim and provides clear reasons and evidence (facts and details) for the argument; organizing writing by grouping related ideas together to support point of view and include a concluding section or statement. • Support counterarguments with logical reasoning and relevant evidence. • Work with a peer or adult to respond to questions, suggestions, or clarification to strengthen the writing. • Participate in individual, shared, and group writing projects, inquiry, and research through investigation and inquiry.	

Writing • Look-For Bank

LOOK-FOR CATEGORIES	GRADE 6	GRADE 7	GRADE 8
Composition (cont.)	• With argument writing, state a claim and provide clear reasons and evidence (i.e., facts and details) for it; organize writing by grouping related ideas to support the claim and including a concluding section or statement.	• Quote and paraphrase data and conclusions from other sources while avoiding plagiarism. • Follow standard formats for citations. • Work with peers and adults to strengthen writing as needed through the writing process, or by trying a new approach, focusing on how well purpose and audience have been addressed.	
	• Brainstorm, draft, revise, edit, and polish writing. • With explanatory, descriptive, or informative writing, introduce a topic and use details and definitions to develop it; include a concluding statement or section. • With narrative writing, establish a situation real or imagined and introduce a narrator and/or characters; sequence unfolds naturally. • Organize and develop the piece well; include a conclusion that brings closure to the experience, event, or plot. • Develop topics with facts, definitions, quotes, and information from reliable sources. • Connect ideas and information, using linking words and phrases. • Organize explanatory, descriptive, or informative writing logically and include headings, illustrations, and multimedia. • Organize opinion writing logically and include reasons to support opinions, supported by facts and details.	• Explanatory, description, or informative writing introduces a topic, examines a topic, and convey ideas, concepts, and information through the selection, organization, and analysis of relevant content. • Reason to support argument are logically ordered and supported by reasons and evidence. • Establish and maintain a formal style.	• Explanatory, descriptive, or informative writing introduces a topic, examines a topic, and conveys ideas, concepts, and information through the selection, organization, and analysis of relevant, well-chosen facts, definitions, details, and other concepts. • Logically support arguments with reasons and evidence. • Acknowledge counterarguments in argument writing.
Mechanics	• Use all types of pronouns clearly. • Recognize fragments and run-on sentences. • Use conventional spelling and consult resources as necessary. • Use underlining, quotation marks, or italics to indicate titles of works.		

Writing • Look-For Bank

LOOK-FOR CATEGORIES	GRADE 6	GRADE 7	GRADE 8
Mechanics (cont.)	• Use punctuation for effect and to separate items in a series. • Use commas to separate introductory phrases and other elements from the rest of the sentence. • Use commas to set apart specific words in a sentence. • Use correlative conjunctions. • Use correct punctuation, including commas and quotation marks. • Express self in simple and compound sentences, and other sentence types.	• Use varied sentence lengths and sentence types to indicate different relationships among ideas. • Express self in complete and complex sentences, rearranging sentences to add clarity to writing.	
		• Use correct punctuation, including commas and quotation marks; use a comma to separate coordinate adjectives. • Place phrases and clauses within a sentence, recognizing and correcting misplaced and dangling modifiers.	• Use correct punctuation, including commas and quotation marks and use punctuation for effect and to separate items in a series. • Use commas to separate coordinate adjectives.

Word Work • Look-For Bank

LOOK-FOR CATEGORIES	KINDERGARTEN	GRADE I	GRADE 2
Environment		• An up-to-date sound wall is present, which students can refer to when reading and writing.	
Phonological Awareness	• Recognize and produce rhyming words. • Identify the number of words in spoken sentences. • Segment syllables in spoken words. • Blend onset and rimes into spoken words. • Change or extend simple single-syllable words by adding or substituting phonemes.		
	• Pronounce syllables in spoken words. • Count syllables in spoken words. • Blend syllables into spoken words. • Break single-syllable words into onset and rime. • Isolate and pronounce initial phonemes in CVC words (e.g., *cat*). • Isolate and pronounce medial phonemes in CVC words. • Isolate and pronounce final phonemes in CVC words.	• Count and pronounce phonemes in spoken words. • Blend phonemes into spoken words. • Isolate and pronounce initial, medial, and final phonemes in single-syllable words. • Blend phonemes, including consonant blends, into spoken words.	
Phonics	• Distinguish between similarly spelled words by identifying different sounds of letters. Segment sounds to write words		
	• Make one-to-one letter-sound correspondences for consonants and vowels in words with regular spellings. Segment and blend CVC words (e.g., *dog*). Segment sounds to read new words. Blend sounds to read new words.	• Read level-appropriate irregular, but common words. Self-monitor and apply word-reading skills to self-correct. Distinguish long and short vowels in regular one-syllable words (CVC and CVCe words).	
		• Decode (segment and blend) single-syllable words. Decode (segment and blend) two-syllable words by breaking them into syllables. Make sound-spelling connections with common consonant digraphs (e.g., *th*) and blends (e.g., *st*).Blend onsets and rimes. Decode long-vowel sounds in regularly spelled one-syllable words (final *-e* and common vowel teams). Know that every syllable in a word must have a vowel sound. Read words with inflectional endings (e.g., *-s, -er, -ing*).	• Know sound-spelling correspondences for common vowel teams. Decode (segment and blend) two-syllable words with long vowels. Decode words with prefixes and suffixes. Identify words with inconsistent but common sound-spelling correspondences
Fluency	• Read and write common high-frequency words and sight words.		
	• Read with fluency (i.e., phrasing and expression). Read emergent texts with understanding.	• Read appropriate texts with purpose and meaning. Read appropriate texts with accuracy and adequate rate and expression to support comprehension. Reread and use context to confirm or self-correct word recognition and understanding.	

Word Work • Look-For Bank

LOOK-FOR CATEGORIES	GRADE 3	GRADE 4	GRADE 5
Environment	• An up-to-date word wall with new vocabulary is present. • An up-to-date word bank with prefixes and suffixes is present.		
	• An up-to-date sound wall is present, which students can refer to when reading and writing.		
Phonics	• Identify and know the meaning of common prefixes and derivational suffixes (i.e., suffixes that make [derive] new words.) • Decode words with common Latin suffixes. • Decode (segment and blend) multisyllabic words. • Segment words into syllables to spell them. • Read level-appropriate irregular, but common words. • Self-monitor and apply word-reading skills to self-correct. • Distinguish long and short vowels in regular one-syllable words (CVCe words).	• Use grade-level phonics and word-analysis skills in decoding words. • Use knowledge of all letter-sound correspondences to decode unfamiliar multisyllabic words in context and out of context. • Use knowledge of syllabication patterns to decode unfamiliar multisyllabic words in context and out of context. • Use knowledge of prefixes, suffixes, and root words to decode unfamiliar multisyllabic words in context and out of context. • Build words using Latin and Greek roots, prefixes, and suffixes.	
Fluency	• Read appropriate texts with purpose and meaning. • Read appropriate texts with accuracy and adequate rate and expression to support comprehension. • Reread and use context to confirm or self-correct word recognition and understanding.		

Word Work • Look-For Bank

LOOK-FOR CATEGORIES	GRADE 3	GRADE 4	GRADE 5
Environment	• An up-to-date word wall with new vocabulary is present. • An up-to-date word bank with prefixes and suffixes is present.		
Phonics	• Use grade-level phonics and word-analysis skills in decoding words. • Use knowledge of all letter-sound correspondences to decode unfamiliar multisyllabic words in context and out of context. • Use knowledge of syllabication patterns to decode unfamiliar multisyllabic words in context and out of context. • Use knowledge of prefixes, suffixes, and root words to decode unfamiliar multisyllabic words in context and out of context. • Build words using Latin and Greek roots, prefixes, and suffixes.		
Fluency	• Read appropriate texts with purpose and meaning. • Read appropriate texts with accuracy and adequate rate and expression to support comprehension. • Reread and use context to confirm or self-correct word recognition and understanding.		

Language • Look-For Bank

LOOK-FOR CATEGORIES	KINDERGARTEN	GRADE 1	GRADE 2
Environment	• Words are discussed regularly and posted around the room. • An up-to-date word wall is present, which students can refer to as they read and write. • Student-made books, charts, and other materials display words and word meanings. • Talk is encouraged. Teacher responds to what students are saying, rather than correcting how they are saying it.		
Listening and Speaking	• Participate in shared language experiences. • Agree and disagree during conversations. • Playfully manipulate language (e.g., deliberate rhyming, making up silly sentences). • Ask and answer questions for the purpose of learning something (including during and after reading). • Talk about what they are reading and writing. • Participate in group conversations by listening to others, taking turns speaking, signaling understanding by agreeing, disagreeing, or commenting appropriately. • Speak using simple and compound sentences to express details. • Listen to books read aloud. • Give and receive feedback by asking questions or making comments. • Listen to others and take turns talking. • Speak audibly and independently. • Teacher discusses confusing points or misunderstandings about the text. • Teacher discusses new or confusing vocabulary and encourages inferences.		
	• Describe familiar people, places, things, and events. • Provide details with prompting and support.	• Express ideas using a variety of sentence types: simple, compound, complex. • Demonstrate listening comprehension in recalling information and responding to instruction. • Teacher respects the child's language or dialect and understands that it reflects the identities, values, and experiences of the child's family and community.	
		• Describe a scene from a book in increasing detail. • Use complete sentences independently or when prompted by an adult.	• Ask for clarification and further explanation about topics and texts in a discussion. • Recount stories and personal experiences with appropriate facts and descriptive details. • Ask for clarification of confusing or unfamiliar information during a read-aloud, shared reading, lesson, or student presentation. • Use complete sentences when discussing, presenting, and responding.

Language • Look-For Bank

LOOK-FOR CATEGORIES	KINDERGARTEN	GRADE I	GRADE 2
Vocabulary	• Use words and phrases acquired from conversation, reading, and being read to. • Ask questions about new words and participate in conversations about words and word meanings. • Learn multiple meanings of words and use words accurately when speaking. • Use common inflections and affixes to understand word meaning. • Explore word meanings and nuances in meaning. • Participate in shared, small-group, and independent reading because reading develops vocabulary.		
	• Attend to word meanings and relationships between words based on concepts. • Use words to identify and describe, making connections between words and their use.		
	• Use frequently occurring nouns and verbs. • Form regular plural nouns. • Use the most frequently occurring prepositions. • Distinguish shades of meaning among spoken words. • Attend to the concepts of word meanings (i.e., instruction focuses on developing word concepts, not just definitions). • Identify real-life connections between words and their use.	• Use sentence-level context clues to determine the meaning of words.	
		• Distinguish shades of meaning among verbs (*jump, leap, hop*) and adjectives (*big, large, gigantic*). • Use common conjunctions to signal simple relationships.	• Use the past tense of common irregular verbs. • Use adjectives and adverbs to modify nouns or verbs. • Use frequently used conjunctions to signal simple relationships. • Understand how word meaning changes when a prefix is added (e.g., *happy, unhappy*). • Use root words to determine the meaning of new words. • Use word parts to determine the meaning of compound words. • Use shades of meaning words. • Describe how words create rhythm in a text (e.g., repeated phrases, alliteration). • Acquire and use words from conversation, reading, and being read to, including general academic and content-specific words.

Language • Look-For Bank

LOOK-FOR CATEGORIES	KINDERGARTEN	GRADE 1	GRADE 2
ELD for English Learners	• Teacher allows students to respond in ways appropriate to their language-acquisition level. • Teacher models language and responds to students' attempt at language, rather than corrects students. • Teacher allows wait time for students to respond when prompted. • Teacher creates a classroom atmosphere that is supportive and nurturing of students' attempt at language use. • Teacher provides abundant written language in the classroom, which is visible to students. • Teacher contextualizes language through pictures, images, video, books, text, pantomiming, and drawing. • Teacher uses strategies that accommodate various behavioral and interaction styles; teaching is culturally competent and respectful. • Teacher differentiates instruction for students at varying levels of language acquisition: beginning, intermediate, advanced, advanced high. • Teacher provides texts and topics that reflect students' races, cultures, and identities. • Teacher systematically develops phonemic awareness and decoding skills. • Teacher builds vocabulary knowledge in the context of classroom work, at every opportunity. • Teacher offers shared and guided learning experiences that provide opportunities to learn new words in English and talk about how they are used. • Teacher focuses on meanings of words, as well as concepts and ideas related to those words, not just definitions. • Teacher explicitly teaches how to read for understanding.		

Language • Look-For Bank

LOOK-FOR CATEGORIES	GRADE 3	GRADE 4	GRADE 5
Environment	• Words are discussed regularly and posted around the room. • An up-to-date word wall is present, which students can refer to as they read and write. • Student-made books, charts, and other materials display words and word meanings. • Talk is encouraged. Teacher responds to what students are saying, rather than correcting how they are saying it.		
Listening and Speaking	• Participate in group conversations by listening to others, taking turns speaking, signaling understanding by agreeing, disagreeing, or commenting appropriately. • Speak using simple and compound sentences to express details. • Listen to books read aloud. • Give and receive feedback by asking questions or making comments. • Listen to others and take turns talking. • Speak audibly and independently. • Teacher discusses confusing points or misunderstandings about the text. • Teacher discusses new or confusing vocabulary and encourages inferences. • Express ideas using a variety of sentence types: simple, compound, complex. • Demonstrate listening comprehension in recalling information and responding to instruction. • Teacher respects the child's language or dialect and understands that it reflects the identities, values, and experiences of the child's family and community. • Ask for clarification of confusing or unfamiliar information during a read-aloud, shared reading, lesson, or student presentation. • Use complete sentences when discussing, presenting, and responding.		
	• Participate in shared language experiences. • Agree and disagree during conversations. • Playfully manipulate language (e.g., deliberate rhyming, making up silly sentences). • Ask and answer questions for the purpose of learning something (including during and after reading). • Talk about what they are reading and writing. • Ask for clarification and further explanation about topics and texts in a discussion. • Recount stories and personal experiences with appropriate facts and descriptive details.	• Participate in shared language experiences about increasingly complex topics, ideas, and information. • Come prepared for group discussions and explicitly refer back to the texts during the discussion, as necessary. • Ask questions to clarify information and ideas and respond to questions that refer to reading and writing. • Contribute to group conversations, ask and answer questions, and elaborate on remarks of other students. • Report on topic or information and describe fictional stories and personal experiences with appropriate facts and descriptive details. • Differentiate between occasions to use formal and informal language.	
		• Listen during discussions and add thoughts and understandings. • Paraphrase text read aloud and information presented in diverse formats and media. • Identify and describe the reasons and evidence a speaker provides to support his or her points.	• Draw conclusions in light of knowledge gained from discussions. • Summarize a written text presented aloud or information presented in diverse media formats.

Language • Look-For Bank

LOOK-FOR CATEGORIES	GRADE 3	GRADE 4	GRADE 5
Vocabulary	• Learn multiple meanings of words and use words accurately when speaking. • Use common inflections and affixes to understand word meaning. • Explore word meanings and nuances in meaning. • Participate in shared, small-group, and independent reading because reading develops vocabulary.		
	• Use comparative and superlative adjectives and adverbs. • Acquire and use accurately grade-appropriate conversational, general academic, and domain-specific words and phrases, including those that signal spatial and temporal relationships. • Use sentence-level context clues to determine the meaning of words. • Use words and phrases acquired from conversation, reading, and being read to. • Ask questions about new words and participate in conversations about words and word meanings.	• Use context as a clue to the meaning of new and multiple-meaning words. • Demonstrate understanding of figurative language, including metaphors and similes. • Use Greek and Latin roots, affixes, and suffixes to determine the meaning of new words. • Describe the meaning of common idioms, adages, and proverbs. • Use the relationship between words (synonyms, antonyms, homographs) to better understand the words. • Ask questions about new words and participate in conversations. • Ask questions about words and word meaning, including academic vocabulary and content-(domain) specific words. • Recognize fragments and run-on sentences.	
		• Use relative pronouns. • Use progressive verb tense. • Use adjectives and adverbs appropriately in sentences and order them according to conventional patterns (prepositional phrases). • Correctly use easily confused words (e.g., *two*, *to*, *too*). • Acquire and use accurately grade-appropriate general academic and domain-specific words and phrases, including those that signal precise actions, emotions, or states of being (e.g., *quizzed, whined, stammered*) and that are basic to a particular topic (e.g., *wildlife, conservation*, and *endangered* when discussing animal preservation).	• Acquire and use accurately grade-appropriate general academic and domain-specific words and phrases, including those that signal contrast, addition, and other logical relationships (e.g., *however, although, nevertheless, similarly*). • Use perfect form of verb tenses (e.g., I had walked, I have walked). • Use verb tense to convey various times, sequences, states, and conditions; recognize inappropriate use of verb tenses. • Use correlative conjunctions.

Language • Look-For Bank

LOOK-FOR CATEGORIES	GRADE 3	GRADE 4	GRADE 5
ELD for English Learners	• Teacher allows students to respond in ways appropriate to their language-acquisition level. • Teacher models language and responds to students' attempts at language, rather than corrects students. • Teacher allows wait time for students to respond when prompted. • Teacher creates a classroom atmosphere that is supportive and nurturing of students' attempt at language use. • Teacher provides abundant written language in the classroom, which is visible to students. • Teacher contextualizes language through pictures, images, video, books, text, pantomiming, and drawing. • Teacher uses strategies that accommodate various behavioral and interaction styles; teaching is culturally competent and respectful. • Teacher differentiates instruction for students at varying levels of language acquisition: beginning, intermediate, advanced, advanced high. • Teacher provides texts and topics that reflect students' races, cultures, and identities. • Teacher systematically develops phonemic awareness and decoding skills. • Teacher builds vocabulary knowledge in the context of classroom work, at every opportunity. • Teacher offers shared and guided learning experiences that provide opportunities to learn new words in English and talk about how they are used. • Teacher focuses on meanings of words, as well as concepts and ideas related to those words, not just definitions. • Teacher explicitly teaches how to read for understanding.		

Language • Look-For Bank

LOOK-FOR CATEGORIES	GRADE 6	GRADE 7	GRADE 8
Environment	• Words are discussed regularly and posted around the room. • An up-to-date word wall is present, which students can refer to as they read and write. • Student-made books, charts, and other materials display words and word meanings. • Talk is encouraged. Teacher responds to what students are saying, rather than correcting how they are saying it.		
Listening and Speaking	• Participate in shared language experiences about increasingly complex topics, ideas, and information, building on others' comments and clearly expressing themselves. • Give and receive feedback by asking questions or making comments. • Come prepared for group discussions and explicitly refer back to the texts during the discussion, as necessary. • Contribute to group conversation, ask and answer questions during the discussion, and elaborate on the remarks of other students. • Differentiate between occasions to use formal and informal language and adapt speech as appropriate.		
	• Participate in group conversations by listening to others, taking turns speaking, signaling understanding by agreeing, disagreeing, or commenting appropriately. • Ask for clarification of confusing or unfamiliar information during a read-aloud, shared reading, lesson, or student presentation.		
	• Speak using simple and compound sentences to express details. • Listen to books read aloud. • Listen to others and take turns talking. • Speak audibly and independently. • Teacher discusses confusing points or misunderstandings about the text. • Teacher discusses new or confusing vocabulary and encourages inferences. • Express ideas using a variety of sentence types: simple, compound, complex. • Demonstrate listening comprehension in recalling information and responding to instruction. • Teacher respects the child's language or dialect and understands that it reflects the identities, values, and experiences of the child's family and community.	• Students' language or dialect is respected and it is understood that it reflects the identities, values, and experiences of the child's family and community. • Participate effectively in a range of collaborative discussions (one-on-one, in groups, and teacher-led) with diverse partners. • Produce and expand complex sentences to express details orally. • Acknowledge when new information is presented by others and when others modify their views. • Ask questions that elicit elaboration of ideas to respond to others' thinking, probing others to reflect on their ideas during discussion. • Explain how ideas presented in diverse media and formats clarify a topic, text, or issue under study. • Express self in complete and complex sentences. • Summarize information from texts read aloud or from presentations and viewing multimedia. • Summarize key points of a speaker and the attitude of the speaker, evaluating the soundness of reasons and relevance of evidence. • Present claims and findings emphasizing salient points in a focused and cohesive manner with relevant evidence, valid reasoning, and well-chosen details. • Include multimedia components and visual displays in presentations to clarify claims and findings and emphasize salient points. • Use complete sentences when discussing, presenting, or responding; report/present opinions and information.	

Language • Look-For Bank

LOOK-FOR CATEGORIES	GRADE 6	GRADE 7	GRADE 8
Listening and Speaking (cont.)	• Paraphrase key ideas expressed to demonstrate understanding of multiple perspectives. • Interpret information presented in diverse media and formats and explain how it contributes to a topic. • Use complete sentences when discussing, presenting, and responding. • Ask questions to clarify information and ideas and respond to questions that refer to reading and writing. • Report on topic or information and describe fictional stories and personal experiences with appropriate facts and descriptive details.	• Delineate a speaker's argument and specific claims and attitude toward the subject, evaluating the soundness of the reasoning and the relevance and sufficiency of the evidence. • Present claims and findings (e.g., argument, narrative, summary presentations), emphasizing salient points in a focused, coherent manner with pertinent descriptions, facts, details, and examples.	• Delineate a speaker's argument and specific claims, evaluating the soundness of the reasoning and relevance and sufficiency of the evidence and identifying when irrelevant evidence is introduced. • Present claims and findings (e.g., argument, narrative, response to literature presentations), emphasizing salient points in a focused, coherent manner with relevant evidence, sound, valid reasoning, and well-chosen details.
Vocabulary	• Ask questions about words and word meaning, including academic vocabulary and content (domain) specific words. • Participate in shared, small-group, and independent reading because reading develops vocabulary. • Recognize fragments and run-on sentences. • Acquire and use accurately grade-appropriate general academic and domain-specific words and phrases; gather vocabulary knowledge when considering a word or phrase important to comprehension or expression.		
	• Use perfect form of verb tenses (e.g., I had walked, I have walked). • Use verb tense to convey various times, sequences, states, and conditions; recognize inappropriate use of verb tenses.	• Learn new meanings for words and use words accurately orally. • Use common, grade-appropriate Greek and Latin affixes and roots as clues to meaning of words. • Understand figurative language and explore word meanings and nuances in meaning. • Verify preliminary determination of meaning of word or phrase. • Use relationship between particular words to better understand each word (synonyms/antonyms, analogies). • Distinguish between connotation (associations) of words with similar denotations (definitions). • Use context (e.g., the overall meaning of a sentence or paragraph; a word's position or function in a sentence) as a clue to the meaning of a word or phrase. • Interpret figures of speech.	

Language • Look-For Bank

LOOK-FOR CATEGORIES	GRADE 6	GRADE 7	GRADE 8
Vocabulary (cont.)	• Use correlative conjunctions. • Use context as a clue to the meaning of new and multiple-meaning words. • Demonstrate understanding of figurative language, including metaphors and similes. • Use Greek and Latin roots, affixes, and suffixes to determine meaning of new words. • Describe meaning of common idioms, adages, and proverbs. • Use the relationship between words (synonyms, antonyms, homographs) to better understand the words. • Learn multiple meanings of words and use words accurately when speaking. • Use common inflections and affixes to understand word meaning. • Explore word meanings and nuances in meaning.	• Determine or clarify the meaning of unknown and multiple-meaning words and phrases.	
ELD for English Learners	• Teacher allows students to respond in ways appropriate to their language-acquisition level. • Teacher models language and responds to students' attempt at language, rather than corrects students. • Teacher allows wait time for students to respond when prompted. • Teacher creates a classroom atmosphere that is supportive and nurturing of students' attempts at language use. • Teacher provides abundant written language in the classroom, which is visible to students. • Teacher contextualizes language through pictures, images, video, books, text, pantomiming, and drawing. • Teacher uses strategies that accommodate various behavioral and interaction styles; teaching is culturally competent and respectful. • Teacher differentiates instruction for students at varying levels of language acquisition: beginning, intermediate, advanced, advanced high. • Teacher provides texts and topics that reflect students' races, cultures, and identities. • Teacher systematically develops phonemic awareness and decoding skills. • Teacher builds vocabulary knowledge in the context of classroom work, at every opportunity. • Teacher offers shared and guided learning experiences that provide opportunities to learn new words in English and talk about how they are used. • Teacher focuses on meanings of words, as well as concepts and ideas related to those words, not just definitions. • Teacher explicitly teaches how to read for understanding.		

Reflection Sheets

Read-Aloud Reflection Sheet

	MY REFLECTIONS	WHAT COULD I CHANGE OR IMPROVE?
I understand that one purpose of a read-aloud is to develop listening and thinking skills, not simply to just "read a book aloud."		
I make sure students don't stay silent during the read-aloud and I evenly distribute opportunities to talk amongst all students.		
I strategically use think-alouds and modeling to model expert thinking about books.		
I select appropriate text to model some aspect of reading or thinking.		
I choose texts appropriate to content being learned that reflect students' interests.		
I choose culturally relevant texts that mirror and window my students and me in our myriad of identities (heritage, race, culture, gender, etc.) and lived experiences.		
I consider students' social-emotional development, including their experiences with trauma when choosing a read-aloud.		
I choose strong text that can also be mentor text during writing instruction.		
I preview text before reading it aloud to plan stopping points for discussion.		
When reading aloud, I model fluency, including reading with intonation and expression.		
I am clear in my goals and objectives for the read-aloud.		

	MY REFLECTIONS	WHAT COULD I CHANGE OR IMPROVE?
I explicitly model, as appropriate, my goals for instruction in fluency appropriate to my grade level (see the Look-For Bank).		
I discuss and model the goals for comprehension instruction appropriate to my grade level (see the Look-For Bank).		
I am a teacher in grades K–2, and I stop reading from time to time and ask *who, what, why, when,* and *where* questions.		
I am a teacher in grades 3–8, and I stop reading from time to time to ask deep comprehension questions (see the Look-For Bank).		
During text discussion, I am a facilitator; students do the majority of the talking.		
I stop and think aloud about confusing points or misunderstandings about the text.		
I stop and discuss unknown or confusing vocabulary and encourage students to make inferences to understand word meaning.		
I make sure students are speaking audibly and with independence.		
I facilitate collaborative conversations about text, story, and nonfiction topics.		

References: Easley, 2004

Shared Reading Reflection Sheet

	MY REFLECTIONS	WHAT COULD I CHANGE OR IMPROVE?
I strategically use think-alouds and modeling to model expert thinking about books.		
I select appropriate text to model some aspect of reading or thinking.		
I choose texts appropriate to content being learned that reflect students' interests.		
I choose culturally sensitive texts that celebrate my students' race, ethnicity, and backgrounds.		
I consider students' social-emotional development, including their experiences with trauma when choosing a read-aloud.		
I choose complex texts; texts, books, or chapters that are longer and more difficult than what the students can read independently.		
I make sure students have a copy of the text, or can clearly see the entire text during the reading.		
As appropriate, I annotate the text with students' guidance and during my think-alouds and modeling.		
I encourage students to annotate their own text.		
I keep the shared reading at the pace of learning to make sure students are cognitively engaged in the discussion and understand the conversation.		
I preview text before reading it aloud to plan stopping points for discussion.		

	MY REFLECTIONS	WHAT COULD I CHANGE OR IMPROVE?
I understand that a read-aloud can be a close reading of text.		
I am clear in my goals and objectives for the shared reading.		
I am a grade K–1 teacher. I explicitly model, as appropriate, my goals for concepts about print instruction as appropriate to my grade level (see the Look-For Bank).		
I am a grade K–3 teacher. I explicitly model, as appropriate, my goals for concepts about phonemic awareness as appropriate to my grade level (see the Look-For Bank).		
I am a grade K–3 teacher. I explicitly model, as appropriate, my goals for concepts about phonics as appropriate to my grade level (see the Look-For Bank).		
I am a grade 4–8 teacher. I explicitly model, as appropriate, using phonics skills to decode new and unknown words (see the Look-For Bank).		
I explicitly model, as appropriate, my goals for concepts about grammar and language use as appropriate to my grade level (see the Look-For Bank).		
I explicitly model, as appropriate, my goals for concepts about comprehension as appropriate to my grade level (see the Look-For Bank).		

	MY REFLECTIONS	WHAT COULD I CHANGE OR IMPROVE?
I model using text structure to deepen comprehension of texts.		
I model using text features to enhance comprehension and facilitate learning of concepts and academic vocabulary.		
I model closely viewing the illustrations in text and discuss how illustrations add to meaning.		
I make sure students are central to the discussion and do the majority of thinking and talking about texts.		
I facilitate for students the guidelines of discussion, including listening to others and taking turns talking.		
I model and provide scaffolding for students to add on to another student's comments.		
During text discussion, I am a facilitator; students do the majority of the talking.		
I stop and think out loud about confusing points or misunderstandings about text.		
I stop and discuss unknown or confusing vocabulary words and encourage students to make inferences to understand word meaning.		
I make sure students are speaking audibly and with independence.		

Small-Group and Independent Reading Reflection Sheet

	MY REFLECTIONS	WHAT COULD I CHANGE OR IMPROVE?
I understand that the purpose of small-group reading is to achieve independent readers.		
I meet with students in small groups for reading.		
Based on student assessment, I create small groups based on small-group reading, transitional small-group reading, or facilitated book clubs.		
I select appropriate text that is a stretch beyond what students can read independently without support.		
I choose texts that reflect students' interests, race, ethnicities, and backgrounds.		
I make sure each student has a copy of the text.		
I begin with phonemic awareness, phonics, word work, or fluency skills (see Look-For Bank).		
I teach comprehension strategies for student use during reading at the table with me (see Look-For Bank).		
I encourage independent reading during small-group time with me there listening to students and coaching students individually; I discourage round-robin reading.		

	MY REFLECTIONS	WHAT COULD I CHANGE OR IMPROVE?
I facilitate collaborative conversations about text, story, and nonfiction topics.		
I nurture student writing about reading at the reading table, including retelling, summarizing, asking and answering questions, and thinking through writing.		
I facilitate for student discussion guidelines, including listening to others and taking turns talking.		
I model and provide scaffolding for students to add on to another student's comments.		
During text discussion, I am a facilitator; students do the majority of the talking.		
I stop and think out loud about confusing points or misunderstandings about text.		
I stop and discuss unknown or confusing vocabulary and encourage students to make inferences to understand word meaning.		
I ensure students are speaking audibly and with independence.		

Writing Reflection Sheet

	MY REFLECTIONS	WHAT COULD I CHANGE OR IMPROVE?
I have a sacred time block for independent writing after a mini-lesson.		
I model, think aloud, and encourage student thinking during mini-lessons.		
I follow mini-lessons with ample independent writing time.		
During independent writing time I sometimes organize guided writing groups.		
During independent writing time I often confer with students and/or conduct a writing conference.		
I facilitate a whole-group share after independent writing time.		
I encourage writing in different genres and about reading.		
I encourage asking and answering questions in writing in order to write to learn.		
I model and think aloud to make sure that students can compose original writing and generate topics and content for writing.		
I guide students to ask for and give responses to writing, referring explicitly to areas of the writing that need clarity or improvement.		
As appropriate to grade level, I make sure students can write narratives, both personal and fictional and write with narrative elements.		
As appropriate to grade level, I make sure students can write explanatory, descriptive, or informative sentences introducing a topic and providing information.		

Writing Reflection Sheet *continued*

	MY REFLECTIONS	WHAT COULD I CHANGE OR IMPROVE?
As appropriate to grade level, I ensure students can write opinions stating a point of view and providing clear reasons and evidence.		
I am a K–2 teacher, I guide students to encode sounds into words and sentences.		
I am a grade 3–8 teacher, I guide students to write unknown words using known spelling patterns, roots, and affixes.		
I model and encourage the use of precise content-specific vocabulary and a variety of transitional words and phrases.		
I support students' work with peers and/or adults to respond to questions, suggestions, or clarifications to strengthen the writing.		
As appropriate to grade level, I facilitate students to work collaboratively with peers and/or adults to use relevant information from experiences or gather relevant information from print and digital sources, take notes and categorize information, and provide a list of sources when writing.		
I guide students to work with peers or adults to respond to questions, suggestions, or clarifications to strengthen the writing.		
I organize individual, shared, and group writing projects for students to participate in through investigation and inquiry.		

Word Work Reflection Sheet

	MY REFLECTIONS	WHAT COULD I CHANGE OR IMPROVE?
I am a K–2 teacher, and I teach specific skills in phonemic awareness (see Look-For Bank).		
I am a K–2 teacher, and I teach specific skills in phonics (see Look-For Bank).		
I am a K–2 teacher, and I have a sound wall.		
I am a K–3 teacher, and I have a word wall.		
I am a grade 4–8 teacher, and I have a vocabulary wall or word banks.		
I am a K–2 teacher, and I teach students to listen to sounds and manipulate sounds in words.		
I am a K–2 teacher, and I teach students to decode letters into sounds, sounds into words, and words into sentences.		
I am a grade 3–5 teacher, and I teach students to use common and uncommon sound-spelling patterns to decode words.		
I am a grade 3–5 teacher, and I teach students to use root words, prefixes, and suffixes to decode words.		
I teach how to read appropriate texts with accuracy and adequate fluency and phrasing to support comprehension.		
I teach how to reread and use context to confirm or self-correct word recognition and understanding.		

Language Reflection Sheet

	MY REFLECTIONS	WHAT COULD I CHANGE OR IMPROVE?
I make sure students' languages or dialects are respected and understood .		
I make sure students participate in shared language experiences.		
I make sure students participate in group conversations by listening to others, signaling comprehension by agreeing or commenting as appropriate.		
I model and encourage producing and expanding simple and compound sentences to express detail orally.		
I make sure students can agree and disagree during conversation, adding on to others' comments as appropriate.		
I encourage playing with language, including manipulating language (deliberate rhyming, making up silly sentences, and so on).		
I support students asking and answering questions for the purpose of learning something (including during and after reading).		
I model and support students asking for clarification and further explanation regarding confusing or unknown information during a read-aloud, shared reading lesson, or student presentation.		
I create opportunities for students to share and talk about what they are reading or writing.		

	MY REFLECTIONS	WHAT COULD I CHANGE OR IMPROVE?
I create opportunities for students to retell, recount, or summarize fictional stories and personal experiences with appropriate facts and descriptive details.		
I create opportunities for students to give and receive feedback by asking questions or making comments.		
I encourage and model how to express self in complete and compound sentences.		
I encourage and model how to demonstrate listening comprehension in recalling information and responding to instruction.		
I discuss readerly behaviors and model how to listen to books read aloud.		
I encourage and model how to use complete sentences when discussing, presenting, or responding.		
I have a specific time set aside during my literacy block for vocabulary instruction, teaching 8-10 new words per week.		
I understand that teaching vocabulary is about teaching concepts about words.		
I use new words often and plentifully focus on repetition and meaningful use of new words.		

ELD (English Language Development) Reflection Sheet

	MY REFLECTIONS	WHAT COULD I CHANGE OR IMPROVE?
I understand that ELD focuses on developing students' language proficiency levels.		
I respect and honor my students' heritage languages and respect their status as immigrants.		
I understand that students' families are their first language teachers and are partners in their journey to learn English.		
I understand that students' language proficiency develops through rich, real-world, purposeful, and meaningful work through listening, speaking, reading, and writing.		
I create an environment accepting of students at their language level that nurtures their growth through respect and understanding.		
I encourage students to talk with peers in their heritage languages in order to process information and ideas, and to discuss how to respond (in English).		
I encourage a language-rich classroom that is not silent; I understand that students develop language proficiency by talking, speaking, and discussing.		
I understand that students will develop interpersonal language skills before academic language skills; however, students need to be involved in academic language through reading, writing, and thinking.		
I use different teaching strategies to accommodate different behavioral and interaction styles. Teaching is culturally competent and respectful.		

	MY REFLECTIONS	WHAT COULD I CHANGE OR IMPROVE?
I ensure the text and topics discussed reflect students' race, culture, and identities, and those of others.		
I expect students to respond in ways appropriate to their language acquisition level.		
I model language and respond to students' attempts at language rather than correct students.		
I offer wait time for students to respond when prompted.		
My classroom atmosphere is supportive and nurturing of students' developing language use.		
I make sure written language is abundant in the classroom and visible to students.		
I contextualize language through pictures, images, video, books, text, pantomime, and drawing.		
I provide instruction that systematically develops phonemic awareness and the print-sound code.		
I build knowledge of vocabulary in the context of classroom work at every opportunity.		
I provide shared and guided learning experiences to provide opportunities to learn new words in English and talk about how they are used.		
I make sure word instruction is focused on the concepts, ideas, and meanings of the words, not just definitions.		
I ensure reading instruction explicitly teaches how to read for understanding.		
I teach ELD through content topics in literature, science, and social studies.		

Benefit Map

High Benefit

Easy to Implement

Hard to Implement

Low Benefit

Empathy Map

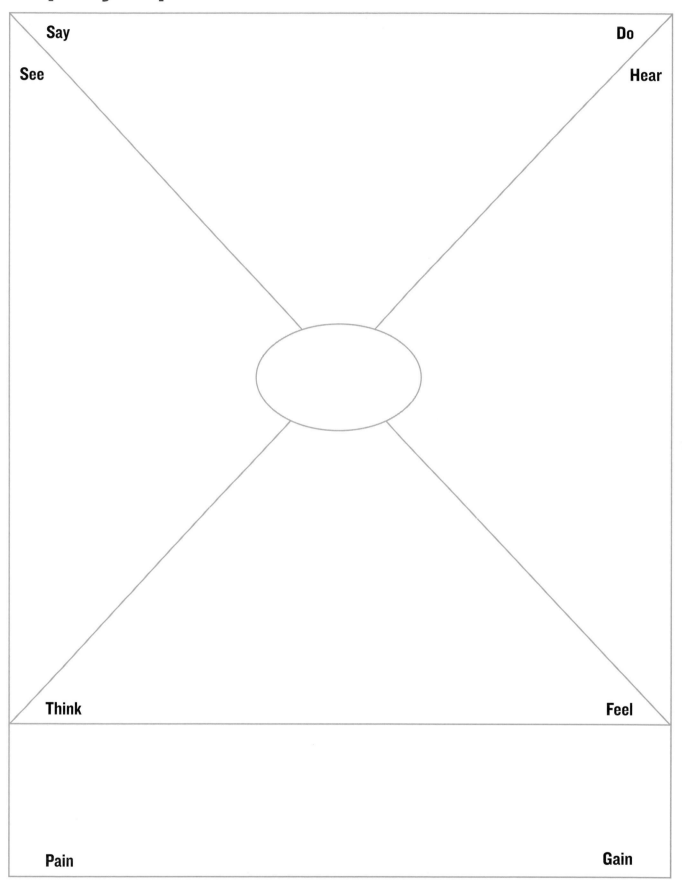

Say

Do

See

Hear

Think

Feel

Pain

Gain

Index

Index: Topics in Look-For Banks

The Look-For Banks can be downloaded at scholastic.com/LiteracyWalksResources.